THE HEART AND ART OF NETWEAVING

THE
HEART
AND ART
OF
NETWEAVING

BUILDING MEANINGFUL

RELATIONSHIPS

ONE CONNECTION AT A TIME

ROBERT S. LITTELL
CHIEF NETWEAVER

Published by

NetWeaving International Press

P.O. Box 11687

Atlanta, Georgia 30355

www.netweaving.com

Printed in the United States of America

1st printing, 2003

ISBN: 1-56352-726-X

Table of Contents

INTRODUCTION

Sometimes it isn't until after a concept has seen the light of day and you have a chance to experience it in operation and watch how people react to it, that you begin to recognize its true nature as well as its real value

So it has been with NetWeaving. My previous book *Power NetWeaving* described the two key skill sets of NetWeaving—serving as a *strategic matchmaker* and acting as a gratuitous *strategic resource provider*—for others. Although the book also provided a structure for improving and expanding these two skill sets, it didn't touch upon what has now revealed itself as the other important element of and the *immediate* payback to NetWeaving.

Artichokes and NetWeaving have something in common. After you peel away the outside layers of the artichoke, you eventually get to the core—the most luscious and appealing part, the heart.

That's what we have discovered about NetWeaving. As we went deeper and deeper in exploring NetWeaving and as we began spreading the word about its "win-win-win" benefits (*win-win* for the two or more persons being connected as well as *win* for the NetWeaver), the closer we got to understanding the real *heart* of NetWeaving.

We used to say that as you act as a *connector* and *resource providers* for others—*with the confidence that what goes around comes around*—it would usually come back around weeks, months, or even years later. Often these rewards are huge. We failed to recognize the IMMEDIATE payback to the NetWeaver in the form of enhanced image, prestige, and empowerment—the kind which can ONLY be generated by helping others.

This book is all about the "heart" of NetWeaving, which is actually the third "win". It involves spreading the word to others and recognizing how it impacts not only the way others perceive you, but even more so watching and enjoying the positive energy force that is generated—for yourself and others—by your NetWeaving activities. This energy will make you better at **everything** you do. If you are in a sales capacity of any kind (which all of us are in one way or another), it will help fortify you against some of the negatives associated with rejection which comes as a part of selling anything—from pots and pans to ideas you're trying to promote.

If you are in management or in an executive position in a company, spreading the word internally—and helping create a NetWeaving culture and environment—will increase your productivity by helping reduce "turf" and other issues in ways you never thought possible.

If by nature, you happen to be more **analytical**, NetWeaving will generate a new brand of satisfaction as you learn how to better "position" yourself as a resource and problem-solver for other's benefit.

When you spread the word to others, it will *inspire* you to want to do **more** as you see the results and outcomes of your ambassadorship.

The first book, *Power NetWeaving*, primarily cited

NetWeaving examples and stories about people in the financial services industry. In fact, NetWeaving is universally practiced within every industry, profession, and academic field. This book celebrates some great examples of people from different fields who recognize not only the value of NetWeaving and who have been doing it over their entire career—just without a word for it—but now find themselves empowered to spread the word about this "**win-win-win-win**" form of networking to others.

It's "**win-win**" for the people who are connected or for whom resources and/or information is provided. It's "**win**" for the NetWeaver who is the "matchmaker" or strategic connector who not only derives "business" benefits from his or her NetWeaving, but a source of energy which only comes from helping others with no hidden agenda. But NetWeaving also supplies a fourth "**win**"—directed toward the community, or the company, or the Chamber of Commerce or any organization (especially charitable) involved where the NetWeaving is taking place and encouraged because NetWeaving is "contagious." The more people doing it, the more people will *want* to do it. (It enriches the entire environment.)

Much of life is all about establishing and developing relationships. What NetWeaving can do, better than anything I've ever seen, is to help each of us establish more **NEW** healthy and fulfilling human relationships. If that doesn't excite and energize you, then you should put this book down and go back to whatever it was you were doing before.

But if this prospect does enthuse and inspire you to read on, you're going to find it rewarding and challenging. The inherent weakness which we've identified with traditional networking, as well as with NetWeaving, when it is only carried to a certain point, is a lack of follow through. NetWeaving offers the electricity to impassion people to want to follow through, but it still will take work. If you want to wake up in the morning with a new sense of energy and *passion* about your work, as well as about helping others while you help yourself, NetWeaving and learning to spread the word about this new concept is just what you've been looking for.

Acknowledgments and Tributes

Whether you're a deeply religious person involved in an organized faith, or just believing in a universe of natural order, there are times in life when many of us feel that there's a *plan* which is guiding us. So it has been with this whole concept of NetWeaving. Rather than create an elaborate strategic plan, I just tried to listen to what I was hearing from people and I connected with those who genuinely wanted to help. I was amazed that every time I needed something or someone, he or she just seemed to appear.

For example, through a connection I made as a result of participating in a panel discussion on networking at the North Fulton Chamber of Commerce, I was introduced to Jack Pilger. Reverend Jack Pilger is a Methodist minister who runs a program at United Methodist Church in Roswell helping persons "in transition" find jobs and help support each other during the search period. Rev. Jack introduced me to several other key people, including Bill Cheeks who, in turn, introduced me to others who have opened a number of doors. This "Tree of Life Connections" continues to grow to this day from that single branch.

And you'll see another one of those trickle-down "branching connections" examples when you read the General Norman Schwarzkopf story describing the most emotional moment I've ever experienced. You'll meet Nancy Richardson and see how my NetWeaving for her in many ways has made this book possible. Through the support of Nancy and others at Xerox, the company has agreed to print this book for free as a show of their support of the concept and their alignment with the NetWeaving philosophy. By their generosity, the entire book price can now become a source of revenue for non-profits and foundations, business and service organizations, and other good causes—especially Junior Achievement—a primary donor recipient. I believe NetWeaving needs to begin with children and young adults, as we teach them that by helping others, in the end, we help ourselves.

Gene Wraith, president of Lincoln Benefit Life, is a good friend and a great human being and was one of the very first supporters of NetWeaving within the financial services industry. He has distributed books to many of their brokers and agents who are in turn telling their clients and prospects about NetWeaving. Also thanks to my many friends and supporters at MIB, the clearinghouse for the insurance industry for life, health, disability, and long-term care insurance. Additionally, my friends Bob Powell, Sr. VP, and John Knowles, VP, Independent Marketing with Jefferson Pilot Financial have likewise agreed to make a contribution whose book purchase proceeds will go to Junior Achievement. Together with others, their financial support is helping us make a major contribution to Junior Achievement right out of the box.

Then there's Steve Massell, Vivian Dubose, and Michael Moore—all past or current presidents of the Buckhead Business Association who bought into the NetWeaving dream and supported it from the very beginning and encouraged me to institute programs still going on to help "weave" NetWeaving into the organization's fabric.

Qin Fan and Janice Rys at the Metro Atlanta Chamber of Commerce first gave us the opportunity to showcase "NetWeaving" at a chamber event and then promoted it heavily within the chamber and became an advocate, asking me to do a series of programs.

And both through the support of Jim Molis, managing editor at the Atlanta Business Chronicle, who wrote a complimentary column about NetWeaving early on, and through Ed Baker's support (publisher and Board Member), as well as Marcia Jaffe's help at the Atlanta Journal and Constitution, the word on NetWeaving is spreading and gaining popularity in a very short time far beyond what I ever dreamed.

I'd be remiss if I didn't also recognize one of my biggest cheerleaders and someone to whom I refer to as my "poster child" of NetWeaving—Mark Schooler in Dallas, Texas, as well as his wife Ann, whose NetWeaving story is included in this book. They truly eat, drink, and sleep NetWeaving 24 hours a day. Mark almost can't finish a conversation with someone without asking, *"And how can I help you?"* And he's genuine when he says it.

And I'd also like to thank Donna Buchanan, executive director of Junior Achievement, as well as Bill Cheeks, retired vice president of training for Equifax and long-time volunteer for Junior Achievement whom I met through Reverend Pilger. Bill is as tireless a NetWeaver as I've ever met. They share my vision of training children and young adults—kindergarten through high school—with a key message of NetWeaving, that one of the best ways to become successful in business and life is helping others become successful.

Thanks also to National Underwriter, the publisher of "Power NetWeaving", for their confidence in me and thanks to my co-author, Donna Fisher. Hopefully readers will also want to read that book to make sure they get down the basic skill sets of NetWeaving, in addition to this book's outline of how to spread the word to others.

I'd also like to give a huge thanks to Jeffrey Gitomer, a popular syndicated columnist and author and speaker who immediately fell in love with the word. He saw it as describing how he has built his business and lived his life. As he put it, he learned at the knee of a NetWeaving great, his own father. I had long respected Jeffrey's masterful, commonsense insights into sales and marketing concepts, and called him after reading one of his columns to run the term by him, not really expecting to see the reception I unleashed.

Probably, though, the defining moment occurred as I was describing one of the two skill sets of NetWeaving—learning how to position yourself as a strategic resource for others, a kind of NetWeaving "Sergeant Bilko." Whether you were a general or a private and whether you needed a part to a jeep that was no longer manufactured, or a date with Marilyn Monroe, you came to Bilko because if he couldn't get it done himself, he would know someone who could. At this point Jeffrey laughed and said, *"You will never guess whose autographed picture I have proudly and prominently displayed in my office—Phil Silvers?"*—

the man who played Sgt. Bilko.

The forward to this book is mostly taken from a column Jeffrey wrote and which appeared in most American Cities Business Journals around the country (October 11-17, 2002).

Also, I'd like to thank a team of people—Michael Moore, Travis Walker, Dr. Carl Proehl, Melvin Dowdell, who have all contributed mightily to moving the project to where it is today. Also much thanks goes to my great friend and attorney, Jeff Scroggin, JD, LLM, who has been my friend, supporter, and my confidante and part-time analyst for many years and who is an distinct exception to the rule about attorneys who are reluctant to NetWeave, for fear of "what could go wrong".

The final tribute is to my lovely wife, Carolyn, who has been my greatest supporter and who is actually a better NetWeaver than I am. But she, like I, is finding the more she talks about it to others and spreads the word, the better she gets. That's what this book is all about.

Apologies to the literally dozens of other people I've failed to mention who have helped me along my NetWeaving journey through introductions, ideas and suggestions they've made which have all been extremely helpful and which will allow this great concept to continue to grow in magnitude and impact. It is true without exception—"Good things happen when good people MAKE things happen."

Foreword

by Jeffrey Gitomer

As an impressionable youth, I watched my dad bring people together that he thought could "do business."

"What do you make, Pop?" I asked.

"Nothing and everything, son. They don't pay me, but I will often be rewarded by them or others in many ways," he said.

"I don't get it, Pop."

"If you give to others without measuring, you get repaid without ever asking for it," he stated as though it were a law of the universe.

"Oh," I said, without really understanding.

"You'll get it later, son," he promised.

My dad repeated his philosophy for years. Helping others at every turn, and bringing people together. And was often rewarded.

By osmosis, I have done the same thing. Never really thought about the right or wrong of it. Never even questioned the validity of it. Just did it. And have often been rewarded. Very often.

Then I came to find that someone had named the process: *NetWeaving*. Bob Littell from Atlanta has even written a book about it. Cool.

Bob invited me to be the guest of honor at two *NetWeaving*

events. One sort of public, held after one of my seminars. And a more private, smaller event held the next evening at a more upscale location.

At the first event, about 150 people were there putting a spin on the traditional "networking" process. "What can I do for you," rather than, "what can you do for me." Great concept. And it worked. After a brief lesson and introduction to the concept of *NetWeaving*, people were engrossed so deeply that no one wanted to leave.

The second, smaller event was held at the fabulous Spa Sydell. An incredible day spa in midtown Atlanta that puts a new meaning to the word "pamper." It's scientific skin care combined with Spa services of every description.

About 50 people of some influence and character (I guess that includes me) came together to see what they could do for one another.

The results were fantastic.

People spent hours trying to involve themselves in others needs. To give of themselves first.

Wanna NetWeave? Start with your BEST. Your best friends, your best contacts, your best influencers, and even your best prospects. Throw a party. Doesn't have to be big. More like a social gathering with a message and a mission: help others first.

The good news is that people who think it's a crazy idea won't show. The better news is that everyone who does show for the event will be eager to participate. The best news is that you will have business and opportunities being thrown at you left and right.

Think about the power of it. In traditional networking, you

show up to "work the room" and try to make a few contacts. At a NetWeaving event, all the people in the room are trying to make connections for you. Wow. Wow.

In a nutshell, NetWeaving is connecting people and positioning yourself as a resource to others—often on a totally gratuitous basis—just with the *belief* to know that "what goes around, comes around."

The interesting part is that when you become involved in NetWeaving, you get into a new business frame of mind. It makes you aware of the needs of others and at the same time challenges you to draw on your full range of contacts. The challenge is as great as the reward.

Like anything else, you have to practice the process outside the event in order to master it. Bob Littell is the current master. He's an insurance guy who doesn't sell insurance. He creates opportunities for other people to succeed, and then people buy from Bob.

Proof? I've seen it personally. And in two events, I've never seen so much power in a room. Not necessarily powerful people, but rather people with the power to help others. It's a business sight to see. And when someone offers their help, you can't help but want to help others.

My philosophy of business has always been "give value first." People read my articles and want more. Been doing that for eleven extremely successful years. Plan to continue that process for the next twenty-five years or so, and then I'll quit. The net result of my column is that I make hundreds of friends by helping them. Friends that one day may turn into business. That's NetWeaving.

"Although I met Bob through some NetWeaving which he did for me that had great impact personally, and professionally in the Insurance & Financial Services industry, myself and others at Xerox Global Services quickly recognized how this concept could equally apply within a business relationship-building context. We have embraced this NetWeaving concept and witnessed it in action, helping stimulate sharing and brainstorming in facilitating our key executive workshops and councils, as well as internally within our company. We are proud to be an important part of this project which we believe will positively impact the entire business community."

— NANCY RICHARDSON, VP, Xerox Global Services, USA

General Norman Schwarzkopf– Nancy Richardson Story

This is my best recollection of what happened at the NAILBA Annual meeting November 17, 2001 during General Schwarzkopf's closing presentation. A version of this was shared with the world. Bill O'Quin, a good friend who sends out the largest email distribution for *Chicken Soup for the Soul*, ended up putting this up on another site he runs for *Reader's Digest*: www.americainuniform.com.

It represents a great example of NetWeaving and the fact that , "what goes around. . .does come back around."

HERE IS THE SCHWARZKOPF STORY

"Norm," as he likes to be called now in his retirement, is into so many humanitarian and charitable activities, it would be difficult naming them all. He may be a retired military General, but like Colin Powell, he represents many of those qualities which are symbolic of the American Spirit. The fact that our military is run by men and women of character and compassion, as well as with a commitment to keep America strong and safe, makes this greatest experiment in humanitarian democracy the world has ever known even more remarkable.

Most of his talk was about leadership. He pointed out that what distinguishes leaders is that they LEAD because they are able to INSPIRE people to WILLINGLY do that which they would not ordinarily do on their own.

It was an incredibly inspirational talk and at the end of his address, he opened things up for Q&A. As you might guess, at this time (November 17—Kabul had just fallen; women were uncovering their faces and men were shaving theirs; the Taliban was in retreat into the South), he was answering many questions about whether or not we should pursue Bin Laden—you already know his answer, and he also contrasted this situation with why we didn't, and why he felt we really couldn't, go after Saddam in the Gulf War.

Just as the session was nearing the end, a young lady came up to the microphone. Although I didn't know it at the time, she was an executive with Xerox, one of the companies exhibiting at the convention. A very attractive and athletic-looking young lady, as she approached the microphone, she held some notes in her hand which she had obviously just scribbled onto a couple of sheets from the notepads provided on the tables in the meeting room.

As she started out, you could hear a slight tremor in her voice and General Schwarzkopf noticed her hands were shaking, which was not surprising in addressing an audience of over 1,000 people. "*Good Morning,*" she finally said, as she looked down at her notes.

Seeing she was a little nervous, and reading from her notes, General Schwarzkopf jokingly asked her, "*Did you memorize that. . .or was that spontaneous?*" She laughed, as did the audience, and that allowed her to regain her composure, and she started reading.

With an ever-increasing inflection in her voice, she described the PRIDE she, her sister and husband who were veterans of the United States Air Force all felt, having served under him, adding that she served in Panama (Air Force—Aircraft Engineer) and as her father before had served in the Army Air Corps. As a request from her father, she thanked General Schwarzkopf for his past and continued leadership.

She also expressed her wish that she could have been in uniform to salute him (military protocol required), while she also regretted that even a handshake wasn't possible because of the added security protection in place in the hall. It had already been announced that Secret Service had been advised to "tackle and subdue" anyone coming within the 40 foot microphone-to-stage-corridor.

She then asked what advice we as parents should give to our children as the next generation of leaders of this country. He said, tell them, "*It's ok to do your own thing, but do it PLUS 1.*" That ONE something extra is to help someone else up a hill; be a leader and stay one step ahead in helping them meet their goals successfully. That's the advice he says he's given his own children.

With her short-read piece completed and answered (probably taking less than a minute), General Schwarzkopf then asked her to come forward to join him on stage.

As she walked the 40 feet to the stage and stood at attention, you could have heard a pin drop. General Schwarzkopf first directed her to salute him and she addressed him with a full military salute, which he immediately returned. After she saluted him, he asked if he could shake her hand. He then asked if he could hug her.

That's when she totally lost it (along with 1,000 other people in the audience) and through her sobs into General Schwarzkopf's lapel-microphone, this audience was treated to an event which will stay in our collective memories for the rest of our lives.

It was an event I shall never forget - one of those once-in-a-lifetime experiences that EVERY person in that room will carry in their hearts, and pass on to their grandchildren. We truly were blessed being in that room and "God Bless America" now takes on special meaning.

But that isn't the REST OF THE STORY.

The meeting was on the Saturday, the week before Thanksgiving. On that following Monday, I happened to be on the phone with Bob Davis, a reporter for *USA Today*, working on another possible story for another consulting client of mine. As we wrapped up our conversation, I told the reporter this story and he asked if I would write it up as an email for him. He wanted to take it to the editors to see if they would print that in the Thanksgiving Day Edition of *USA Today*.

Well, it didn't get published there, but the email, which is very similar to what is described above, literally went around the world as people sent it to friends, and they sent it to friends and family, etc., etc. Then when my friend Bill O'Quin put it up on the www.americainuniform site, military persons around the world were also treated to this great story.

About two weeks later, I received a phone call from Nancy Richardson, the lady with Xerox who had shared her story and emotions. First she thanked me again for all the work I had done and frankly it WAS a lot of work – calls to confirm the facts from her and to get her permission and her willingness to appear in *USA Today* which she was thrilled to do. Then actually writing up the event, as well as a number of calls back and forth with the reporter with *USA Today*, and then later with Bill O'Quin.

But then Nancy apologized for the fact that even though I'd done all this work, she still had never asked me what I did for a living. I told her that I sell some insurance, act as "second opinion" fee-paid consultant to high net worth individuals, as well as serve as a consultant to insurance companies and vendors. As I described more about my background and some of my clients, she said, "*We need to hire you.*" And they did.

AFTERMATH – ALMOST A YEAR LATER

In September of 2002, in Rochester, NY, I helped Xerox put on a very successful meeting which not only added much to their meeting, but it also opened up my eyes to new possibilities for NetWeaving in helping technology companies create an atmosphere of openness and sharing at technology "user group" meetings. As a consequence of that discovery, I have gotten several other engagements which I would not have even considered had it not been for this opportunity—all brought about by NetWeaving.

As we say about NetWeaving, every single act of NetWeaving is like throwing a stone into a still pool of water. It sets off an ever-expanding set of circumstances and chain of events, whose consequences and ramifications may not be known for days, months, or even years into the future. Nevertheless, as sure as the sun also rises, *"what goes around. . .does come back around. . . and good things DO happen. . . when good people MAKE things happen."*

THE LATEST CHAPTER

As a result of my NetWeaving activities for Xerox, and their "buy-in" to the NetWeaving concept, both philosophically as well as in the way they work with their customers, this book was printed as a donation by Xerox.

1

The Skill Sets of NetWeaving Revisited – The NetWeaver's Creed

Do not go where the path may lead,
go instead where there is no path and leave a trail.
— Ralph Waldo Emerson

NetWeaving is a "Golden Rule" form of networking which focuses on helping others first, or at least putting others' needs, problems and opportunities on a more equal plane with those of our own; doing so with the belief and conviction that, over time, *"what goes around, will come back around."*

The Golden Rule is all about helping others: *"Do unto others as you would have them do unto you."* That at least indirectly implies you wouldn't mind if someone returned the favor you've done for them. So it is with NetWeaving. Your motives are first and foremost, to help others, but there's certainly nothing wrong with doing so in ways which increase the chances that the NetWeaver will benefit in the long run. I like to call it, *"enlightened"* self-interest.

The help you provide others comes in two forms:

- Being a strategic connector of other people—helping create "win-win" relationships between two or more other persons, a *strategic matchmaker.*

- Being a *strategic resource provider* for others—helping them find solutions to their needs and problems, as well as ways to help them take advantage of ideas or opportunities they have, but which, without someone else's help, will never materialize into anything of consequence.

One of the most interesting and important discoveries I've made since the first book was released, and since I've matured in my understanding of the concept, is that the "matchmaking" which one does (i.e. connecting other people) as a NetWeaver does not need to be anywhere near as "strategic" as I once thought necessary in order to have a positive impact. I used to overly worry about whether or not these two persons whom I was bringing together would find a good strategic fit so they could discover ways to help each other.

Would the fact that one of them is in this business or industry, and the other person is in this other business or industry, make strategic sense from a standpoint of whether or not they could find ways to be of help to each other?

Would the two persons find things or interests in common or people they both knew and didn't realize and which could help one or both of them?

If I was looking to connect someone in the real estate business with someone else, I would be normally be looking for someone in the potential market to buy a home, or maybe someone who needed or did interior decorating, where they might be able to send business back and forth to each other. But what really began to be clear was that in a majority of the cases, when I'd put almost any two people together, THEY would find some things they had in common, or ways to help each other, outside of the reason I had thought for matching them up.

Although much of the NetWeaving which I and others do, does have some strategic logic behind it, I have found it's not necessary to be overly concerned about whether there's a strategic fit. Just put two creative, talented, interesting, and successful people together and sit back and watch the magic as the positive energy is created and flows. If this is someone you think is interesting and whom you would like to get to know better, so would many other persons benefit from getting to know him or her.

The only real ingredient for NetWeaving to flourish is that both people whom you are connecting need to be people of good character, and have the capacity and the desire to help others, rather than just themselves.

In the absence of these gratuitously generous human qualities, here's what often occurs:

The inwardly focused person whom you connect with someone else will not be actively looking out for ways to help the other person and instead will simply be looking for ways to benefit him or herself (i.e. a taker; not a giver). If the other person who is a "giver" ends up connecting the *taker* with someone or providing resources, the other person (i.e. the taker) will not feel any obligation to worry about returning the favor the NetWeaver did since they're still all about, "*What's in it for ME?*" Unfortunately, when a "taker" recognizes you, as a connector and a "giver," rest assured, they'll be back for more.

That spoils the concept for the "giver" who hopefully will realize he or she just needs to move on when this conclusion seems obvious, which unfortunately is not always easy to recognize.

You won't be able, nor should you try, to "convert" people to becoming NetWeavers. Generally, people either genuinely derive joy and satisfaction from helping others, or they don't. My rule of thumb is, you give, and you give, and give, and when you see nothing coming back, you just go on to help the next person.

Luckily, there are many exceptions to this. In fact, some persons who have been very inwardly focused or driven over much of their lives, convert themselves when they discover NetWeaving and find the joy which comes from helping others, and become passionate about it. They also notice how infectious and contagious it is.

THE SKILL SETS

The skill sets and the qualities of being or becoming a Power NetWeaver include:

- Learning how to create new habits. Learning how to make them permanent. Understanding that even good

NetWeavers can become great NetWeavers with practice.

- Improving your listening and notetaking skills. This is critically important for making your NetWeaving effective and especially for enhancing the chances that good things will happen in return.

- Understanding the importance of followup. Learning to be a better listener and taking better notes will all be for naught if you don't have good follow up.

The first book was about the "how's" of NetWeaving, this book is about the "heart" and "art" of NetWeaving. Learning how to spread the good word about all the positive things that occur with NetWeaving, teaching and mentoring others, or just using the word in everyday conversation, and how this can have a positive impact on your image, your energy, and your business and your personal life, as well as on that of others.

NETWEAVING SKILL SET CHECKLIST

1. Who's the last person you can remember connecting"with another person, primarily with their benefit and welfare in mind?

2. Did you ever follow up to see what the outcome of that introduction turned out to be?

3. Did you ever find out if this introduction possibly ended up with another introduction to a third party . . . or a fourth?

4. Who is the best NetWeaver you know, someone who is constantly connecting other people ? Do you notice that their listening pattern is different, listening for opportunities to connect others and help?

5. Have you ever thought of yourself as a *resource* for others? If yes, what things have you done to *position* yourself as a resource? If no, what things should you be doing, or what could you be doing better to help you develop those skills?

6. How broad and deep of a "resource network" have you established—persons whom you would trust referring to your best client or customer—with the absolute confidence that he or she will give exceptional service and that your image will be enhanced from making the referral? If it's only a few people wide and deep, why haven't you been looking for more persons to become part of your "trusted resource network?"

2

IMAGES AND PERCEPTIONS
CAN BE CHANGED OVERNIGHT

There are those who look at things the way they are, and ask why . . .
I dream of things that never were, and ask why not?
— ROBERT F. KENNEDY

Not long after the original book, *Power NetWeaving,* was released, the tragic events of September 11, 2001, unfolded. In fact, I was scheduled to be making a presentation on NetWeaving that fateful morning to the Professional Women's Round Table in Pomona, California. The meeting organizer did-n't know whether or not to cancel the meeting, but since about 30 women (and one male guest) showed up for the meeting, they voted in favor of having it, and asked me to go ahead and speak. I'm glad I did, because I discovered things at the meeting which helped me recognize the true "heart" of NetWeaving.

Looking back, there was something almost surrealistic about that morning—riveted to the TV in an almost obligatory fashion, feeling compelled to share the grief, watching the scenes on the TV of the airplanes crashing into the twin WTC towers being replayed over and over again. For all practical purposes, the entire country was in a numbed state of shock. It was only several days later, as our horror subsided, that the scope and magnitude of the disaster really began to sink in, and the impact that 9/11 was going to have on our entire lives from that day on.

I ended up stranded that entire week in San Diego, so I had a chance to reflect upon reactions to a number of talks I'd already given on NetWeaving, as well as the feedback and reactions to the book. This, combined with what I'd observed at the meeting in Pomona, helped me begin to recognize what I began to call the "heart" of NetWeaving.

In a way, the events of September 11 exposed the real "heart" of our country. The patriotic national outpouring and a renewed focus on helping others, revealed not only the country's ability to survive tragedy of this magnitude, but it also helped illuminate the benefit that NetWeaving could have for those affected by the tremendous economic ripple effects which would begin to negatively compound what was an already slumping economy.

Firemen have always played a critically important role in our society and have been appreciated to a certain degree. After September 11, there's been marked change in people's attitudes toward firemen. They are now seen in a more "*heroic*" light. You might even say the entire profession of firefighting has been elevated and given a "halo" which makes them all "heroes." Our appreciation rose to near adulation.

And not only was our image of firemen elevated, their own self-image and pride for their profession received a huge boost.

It's not unusual, even today, to see a fire engine on its way to a fire or emergency with a big American flag mounted on top of the firetruck, blowing in the wind.

Out of the dust, the rubble, and the death, and the reaction to those who conceived and perpetrated the deed, there emerged an American spirit that transcended the fear and anger we all experienced. We all felt better seeing that kind of spirit being exhibited by others—the singing of God Bless America wherever we turned, the flags everywhere, our President and Mayor Giuliani exuding a resolve that we will defend our way of life. The attackers may have taken thousands innocent lives and destroyed office space greater than all of downtown and midtown Atlanta, Georgia, combined, but we would endure. They hadn't dented the American spirit and in fact actually they had made us all more resilient and more appreciative for what we have and some of what we had been taking for granted.

New Yorkers who had previously earned a reputation for callous, insensitive behavior, gained a much softer and humane image as a reaction to the countless acts of kindness and bravery being reported. In a somewhat shocking reversal, New York City tied that year with Charleston, South Carolina, for the "friendliest city" in the country.

Another image reversal we saw involved President George W. Bush. In the week prior to the terrorist attacks, he had an approval rating of right around 50%. Within weeks after the event—seeing him standing in the ruins with firemen beside him emotionally touched by the family's collective tragedies, and giving speeches which released a "passion" which theretofore had been clouded and shielded—his approval rating soared to almost 90%. A year later, in spite of a still slumping economy, continuing terrorist uncertainty, as well as an imminent war with Iraq, his rating was very positive.

Images CAN be changed overnight.

I don't want to make any kind of direct comparison between the aftermath halo effect bestowed upon those firemen who rushed into the burning towers to save lives, or the overnight positive image rebound of President Bush, with the image transformation which happens to those who help spread the word about NetWeaving. But there is definitely an enhancement of one's image . . . and in many cases, it's instantaneous. To a somewhat lesser but important degree, we've discovered the real power and the heart behind NetWeaving, involves more than simply being a "NetWeaver" to and for others. It's all about becoming a vocal proponent of and advocate for NetWeaving and helping spread the word of the benefits to others—a NetWeaving ambassador.

Those persons who introduce NetWeaving to others are not only seen in a positive light by others, they create a positive force, the kind that only comes from helping others. This can be as true for someone who introduces the NetWeaving concept to a single individual—connecting two other people—as it is for someone who takes NetWeaving into a company or service organization, helps use it to raise funds for a non-profit or to form a NetWeaving group.

This altruistic concept, which focuses on helping other people solve their problems, fulfill their needs, or capitalize on their opportunities with little or no regard for how the NetWeaver will benefit, earns that person an elevated status, or as we euphemistically refer to it a "halo" for the NetWeaver.

When someone introduces the concept of NetWeaving to an individual, a group of people, or to an entire organization or company, and then helps educate them on the various aspects of NetWeaving, we refer to this broadcasting and mentoring activity as becoming a *"NetWeaving ambassador."* They are representing what NetWeaving is all about and the good it does for others while reflecting positively back on themselves.

And even better news: when more people NetWeave and when everybody NetWeaves more often, it spreads within a group or organization. NetWeaving truly is contagious—the more people do it, the more they enjoy it. And there's a positive energy force associated with NetWeaving, the same kind you find within a group working on a charitable project such as building a house with Habitat for Humanity.

The altruistic nature of NetWeaving involves the notion of helping others with only a *back-of-the-mind* hope that, somewhere down the line, the NetWeaver may benefit. Those who spread this *golden rule* concept inherit a heightened prestige enhancing themselves in the eyes of others, while experiencing an increase in their own self-confidence and sense of pride and accomplishment.

As the time frame from 9/11 widens, many are somewhat disheartened to see our country slipping back into some of our old ways—less overtly patriotic, less flexibile and less caring toward others. NetWeaving can supply a positive reminder for helping others, 365 days a year. We're all human. And, although there are Mother Teresa's in the world whose altruism is pure and without an ounce of self-interest, most of us are not that perfect. How can we be motivated to do good for others on a daily basis—partly out of pure altruism, while at the same time not beating ourselves up for *hoping* that our good deeds will somehow be returned? This includes finding ways to *increase* the chances that our good deeds will come back around to benefit us. NetWeaving involves doing good for others with *enlightened self-interest* in mind. Our motives are to help others but we do so with the confidence and belief in the law of reciprocity—what goes around, will come back around.

In order for someone to become a NetWeaving Ambassador, he or she first must become adept at the NetWeaving skills of being a strategic connector of others The person must also learn how to better position him or herself as a resource for others. I would refer any readers of this book to the first book, "Power NetWeaving."

After these skill sets have been developed and refined (or concurrently while they are being honed), persons can begin practicing some of the aspects of becoming a NetWeaving ambassador. The "art" of NetWeaving involves being both a skilled NetWeaver, as well as an accomplished NetWeaving ambassador.

Here are the five key steps to becoming a NetWeaving ambassador:

1. Memorize or learn to paraphrase the NetWeaver's Creed, which pretty much summarizes what NetWeaving is all about (see "Power NetWeaving" book).

2. Learn the analogy between solving a jigsaw puzzle and NetWeaving (Chapter 4)

3. Learn to explain how NetWeavers train themselves to listen with a second pair of ears and to be tuned in during every conversation with a second set of antennae for solutions to the other person's needs, problems, and opportunities (Chapter 5).

4. Learn how to introduce NetWeaving "one-on-one" to friends, family, neighbors, customers, and prospective customers and clients, and especially how to encourage persons for whom you "host" meetings, and for whom you connect by phone, to do the same thing—Pass It On To Two Others (PIONTTO) what we refer to as a "business version" of the "Pay It Forward" concept (Chapter 8—Referrals and Hosting).

5. Learn how to take NetWeaving into groups and organizations to which you belong and learn how it can create and transform relationships from superficial into meaningful relationships over time (see Chapters 9 and 10 on Creating NetWeaving Cluster Groups and Holding NetWeaving Events).

3

The Primary Weakness Of Traditional Networking— Superficiality

Truth is not always in a well. In fact, as regards the more important knowledge, I do believe that she is invariably superficial. The depth lies in the valleys where we seek her, and not upon the mountain tops where she is found.
— Edgar Allan Poe

One of the first things I noticed as I began making presentations and giving speeches about NetWeaving was the way people seemed to immediately "warm up" to the word and the concept. And often their affection was followed by some remark about their dislike or distaste for networking and/or the concept in general, as being too shallow, manipulative and superficial.

Almost everyone needs more business. The concept of networking which I refer to as *"building a network of contacts and relationships"* is a worthwhile goal for anyone who is in business or just walking through life. What turns most people off about it is the traditional way most people network.

Also some people, especially more analytical types, don't like the idea of doing something they consider to be self-serving.

The way I distinguish the two terms—networking and NetWeaving—is that networking (done correctly) is primarily done with the idea in mind of building or adding to your own network, whereas NetWeaving is based on the concept of helping others build or add to their own network for their benefit. NetWeaving is done with confidence and belief that your actions will eventually benefit you in ways you could never have dreamed possible, with outcomes that far exceed those of traditional networking.

IT'S THE RELATIONSHIPS, STUPID!

It's really not magic or brain surgery. The most successful people in life are not necessarily the smartest. They're aren't even necessarily the ones who are best able to identify person's needs and problems, and suggest or provide solutions. The ones who, almost without exception, end up at the top, are those who know how to build and maintain relationships with others, and the pinnacle of relationship building is "trust".

Getting along with people requires getting to know the other person at a certain acceptance level and to a certain extent, learning, or trying to learn, how to walk in their shoes. But getting to know someone well takes guts because it means breaking through the superficiality existing at most levels of communication.

To some degree, we must recognize that maintaining our distance in initial conversations—staying at a superficial, small-talk level—is a protective mechanism that all of us use to help overcome our initial feelings of awkwardness at meeting new people.

WHAT'S YOUR SIGN IN A BUSINESS CONTEXT?

Back in the 60's and early 70's, the big thing was, "*What's your sign?*" In many ways this was also superficial and shallow, but in some positive ways, it armed people with an opening question which begged for more conversation: "*Oh, so you're a "Gemini? So that must mean you . . . .*"

Nothing is wrong with starting out in small talk and almost any topic which leaves the other end open for the other person to easily respond is a great way to *start* communicating.

The real shortcoming of traditional networking is people tend to remain at this very superficial level and never really break through the ice and get to know the other person. And even when they do **begin** to penetrate the superficiality, too often communication plateaus at a level just below where a meaningful relationship could begin to be formed. The relationship-building process ends.

Too many networking groups and functions are all about having superficial conversations, exchanging business cards, and leaving with a false sense of satisfaction. I call this "*grazing for leads and/or solutions*". People roam around from person to person. . . group to group, have short conversations, try to establish if the other person is a prospect for what they have to offer or if the other person can help solve one of their burning needs or problems. And when they determine there isn't a match with their need or problem, it's on to the next person or the next group.

And even when there seems to be a match and both of you

exchange business cards promising to follow up the next day typically finds each person barely recalling what the other one looked like, let alone the exact nature of the product or service they were offering or the details of the conversation.

Any leads which are exchanged in this environment are almost always *bottom of the barrel*, no-risk. . . ones. These are the names of persons the referrer doesn't consider to be that valuable. If the referral connection doesn't work out, it won't reflect negatively back on them since there wasn't a strong connection in the first place.

The truth is that unless a meaningful relationship begins and until **trust** is established, it's unlikely any leads will be exchanged. And the referrals actually made will generally be of poor quality.

NETWEAVERS HAVE A RIGHT TO BE NOSEY

In order to become a *"power"* NetWeaver, you must become adept at asking probing questions and being a good listener. But also you must have good follow-through skills. Be a good note taker and most importantly, follow up in a timely manner in order to retain the information you've gathered. Follow through in order to move the relationship to the next level.

If you take the attitude you don't want to be considered too nosey by asking too many probing questions, you will probably never become a skilled NetWeaver. When you truly believe in what you're doing and in the value of NetWeaving, the fear goes away because you're on a mission of helping others.

But in order to allow the other person to know your motives and realize that you aren't just trying to be nosey, it's good to preface any penetrating questions with a little description of what NetWeaving is all about.

A typical NetWeaving introduction might go something like this:

NetWeaver: *Steve, have you ever heard the term "NetWeaving?"*

Usually the response will be "*no*" (but that's changing quickly).

NetWeaver: "*NetWeaving is a "Golden Rule" form of networking which puts the other person's interests FIRST, or at least on a more equal plane with our own. A NetWeaver is someone who is constantly looking for ways to connect people, or to supply them with the information or resources they need and doing this because they just enjoy helping other people.*"

Often, the first response from the other person will be something like: "*What a great word. . .or, I've done a lot of that in my time.*" It's good if you can encourage the other person to talk about a situation in which he or she acted as a "*NetWeaver*" because it will help lock the concept into their subconscious.

Now that you've set the stage, you can now say something along these lines:

"*In order for me to be a NetWeaver for you, it would help me if I knew a little more about you. I'll be better able to recognize any-thing which might be a good solution for some of your particular needs, problems, or opportunities."*

WOMEN HAVE AN ADVANTAGE— THEY'RE BETTER NATURAL NETWEAVERS

One day a friend of mine who was familiar with the NetWeaving concept whispered something to me, very humbly, but sincerely. He said, "Bob, you know your wife, Carolyn is a better NetWeaver than you are." And I agreed.

As I was sharing this opinion that women are better natural NetWeavers than men, my wife commented that it was due to women's "nurturing" nature—maybe something biologic and genetic going on there.

On the whole, human beings tend to have to work at becoming social animals. As children, some of us tend to adapt easily on the playground and girls especially seem to form groups. And often while little boys are playing soldiers and building model airplanes or cars, and engaging in other more solitary exercises, little girls are typically engaged in activities which involve more socialization and communication (this is actually changing somewhat as little girls are more often being introduced early on to competitive sports.)

Their higher socialization quotient, combined with their better listening skills and more experience drawing information out of others makes them more natural NetWeavers.

Have you ever thought of what purpose playing games like charades serves? It forces us out of our comfort zone. Sometimes we purposely hang around outrageous people because they say and do things which force us out of our comfortable habits and ways.

These examples show that in traditional networking, most of us tend to stay inside our own comfort zones. We tend to keep the conversations at superficial, "non-threatening" levels, partly because we're on a mission to develop business and we see that as a straight line strategy—"are you a prospect for me?"— but also because it's much easier and less threatening to stay inside our comfort zone.

THE THREE KEY QUESTIONS

In NetWeaving, we like to arm people with three key questions which help people open up in a business context:

1. Tell me how you make your money—not just, what is your business? The better I understand how you actually create revenue in your business, the better I will be able to help you. What does a *best* prospect for you or your business look like? A good way to follow up on this first question is to ask, "Tell me the story of how you landed your biggest account, or landed your best client or customer?" This not only gives you insights into the process he or she goes through to make a sale or create a client. Even more impor-

tant, you will retain the information longer because we remember stories much better than we do facts.

2. In a business, family, or personal context, what is your most *burning* problem, need, or opportunity with which I (we) might be able to help you?

3. What is your "strategic advantage?" As I'm attempting to *sell* you to someone I know, or at least open a door for you, how do I describe you in terms that differentiate you from others doing the same, or nearly the same, thing?

A FEW OTHER QUESTIONS TO BREAK THROUGH THE SUPERFICIALITY

Another one that is interesting, especially as you get to know the person better, is—"If you've reached the point in your life where you've begun to explore more about what your life has meant, and whether you want to leave any kind of a legacy. . . what would that legacy be, and is there any way I can help you create or develop it?"

And how about, *"What's your sign?"* (just wanted to see if you're still paying attention, although it's still not a bad opening line as long as you know your astrology.)

Here's another one that's "fun": *"If you WEREN'T doing what you are today, and assuming money were no object, what would you be doing and why?"* Another way of asking the same thing is, "*What's your passion?*"

SOME ADDITIONAL NETWEAVING EXERCISES

~ Do you agree with the statement that most networking conversations tend to be very superficial?

~ If you agree, why is this? If you don't agree, how have you been able to break through the superficiality which typically exists? Have you been NetWeaving without realizing it?

~ What are some ways to break through the superficiality?

- Learn to listen differently.
- Shift the conversation to something of meaningful substance where people are learning and growing.

- Try introducing the topic of NetWeaving into the conversation and watch how it elevates the dialogue.

- When people understand what NetWeaving is all about, and they see that your intentions are to help, watch how they open up.

4

THE JIGSAW PUZZLE ANALOGY—
WALKING, TALKING JIGSAW PUZZLE

Imagination is more important than knowledge.
— ALBERT EINSTEIN

Think of the last time you walked up behind someone who was working on a a jigsaw puzzle. As you began looking for a possible fit for some of the remaining pieces, you probably spotted the location of a couple of missing pieces which the puzzle solver had overlooked. Why? Because you brought a new perspective to the table along with a different approach to problem-solving. Brain researchers even say the neurons in our brain connect in unique ways and those connections allow each of us to see things differently.

Has someone ever showed you a "Rorschach" sketch of the old woman/young woman and asked you what you see? In a large group, part of the group will swear that it's the nostalgic side-view of a coquettish young lady looking away, hair up in a bun with a scarf tied around her neck. The other group will swear it's a picture of an old hag with a big nose. Instead of a scarf, they see the lines of her mouth.

What's also interesting is that we can only see one perspective at a time. As our eyes begin to focus on the old lady rather than the young woman, we lose sight of the reverse image and the opposite is also true.

The aftermath of this revelation is similar to how we feel when someone points out the obvious fit of a missing piece to the jigsaw puzzle. We have a hard time understanding why we couldn't have seen what they saw.

WE'RE ALL WALKING, TALKING JIGSAW PUZZLES. . .WITH MISSING PIECES

When you get right down to it, each of us is a *"walking, talking jigsaw puzzle"* with some of our pieces missing. Some of these are in the form of *needs* that are going unfulfilled; some are *problems* in need of solutions. Some are *ideas* or *opportunities*. Some hold great promise but which, without help from others—operational, management, or technology expertise; money or moral support—they may never see the light of day, or certainly may never reach their full potential.

Each of these groups of missing pieces—needs, problems, and ideas or opportunities—could fall into the context of a business, family, or personal situation, or, some combination of all three.

A number of years ago, I was asked by the CEO of a company with whom I was doing a lot of business to help some friends who were moving to Atlanta from out of state. He was becoming the new CEO of a large technology company. My wife and I took he and his wife to dinner, drove them around the area to show them several housing possibilities, and referred a realtor to them. Even though they ended up using their own realtor, we stayed in touch.

Guess who was later called when some significant life insurance was needed? This relationship extends to today.

A truly skilled NetWeaver understands a person may not always recognize the need, problem, or opportunity. Sometimes the NetWeaver must act in the role of educator, enlightener, and motivator, and once there is recognition, switch roles to that of the NetWeaver.

The missing pieces can sometimes be found by being introduced to a *person* who can help find the solution. In other cases, it may be *information* or some other *resource* (e.g. a website) which can best solve the puzzle. You should always think of both categories—people as well as information or resources.

FINDING OUR OWN MISSING PIECES— LEARN TO DO DOUBLE-DUTY

It shouldn't be surprising that most us spend our lives simply trying to locate the missing pieces to our own business, family and personal jigsaw puzzles. It's only natural that we would first look out for our own and our family's interests.

NetWeaving encourages us to do double-duty. While we're

out there looking for our own missing pieces, we can train ourselves to be looking for other's at the same time.

We are all uniquely qualified to help other people find the "missing pieces" to their puzzle. A skilled NetWeaver is constantly on the lookout for ways to help persons locate his or her missing pieces: trying to find ways to bring people together in win-win relationships, or providing them with the resources that they may need.

FOCUS IS THE KEY

When you are working on a jigsaw puzzle you are totally focused. You're looking for color and tint matches; for patterns and designs in the shape of the puzzle pieces and in the context of the "big picture" you're trying to re-create.

You're looking for clues of all kinds to locate the missing pieces. The same is true when you're NetWeaving.

Once you have identified someone's need, problem, or opportunity, you go into a problem-solving mode. Solutions are out there for all of our needs, problems, and opportunities, if only we are able to cast our net wide enough to find those most able to help.

QUESTIONS ARE KING

There was a well-known insurance personality, Roger Zener, who used humor as his primary sales tool. It also helped that he looked and sounded like Jonathan Winters, but he had one other saying which may have been more powerful than his humor. He would say, "*When in doubt, ask a question.*"

I would advise young people just coming out of college that learning how to ask questions instead of making statements is the most powerful and effective way to get your point across.

My good friend Amy K. Hutchens, who did her Master's work at John Hopkin's in brain research, tells us that when we ask a question, it puts the person in a different mode than when we make a statement to which someone is simply going to react—yes, no, or maybe:

"*When you ask yourself questions or are asked questions by others, the question itself will trigger your brain's synapses and these synapses will wire and fire to create meaningful connections that provide you with an answer to the question.*" [1]

By forcing ourselves to go through a series of questions as we are attempting to help someone, we personally experience the same process. It triggers new thoughts and modifications of existing ideas which lead us in new directions.

Whenever I'm stumped on any problem or situation, I sit down and start writing as many questions as possible using all the key question words:

who, what, when, why, why not, where, which, will, how, how much, if, if not, does this make sense?

[1] "Brain Brilliant", Amy K. Hutchens (AmyK Publishing International, 2002), p. 42

BECOMING A BETTER CONNECTOR OF OTHER PEOPLE (A STRATEGIC MATCHMAKER)

Here are some other questions which can help you as you're attempting to help others find the missing pieces to business, family, and personal jigsaw puzzles:

- **What are the names of some people whom you would most like to meet?**—You'll be surprised that you may either know him or her, or more likely you may know someone who knows that person well and who can make a favorable introduction.

- **What is the most valuable introduction or connection anyone ever made for you and why?** You should recognize that you have been the recipient of many valuable introductions. If you haven't been on the receiving end, you may want to ask yourself why that is.

- **What are your key interests outside of work and is there someone who would be an interesting contact in that area?** Some of the most interesting connections you will help people make have nothing to do with business initially, but when people find things that they have in common, they tend to bond more quickly and then are open to working together more closely. Why do you think so much business is transacted on the golf course?

- Do you find you have a fairly easy time making meaningful new relationships with your hectic business and family schedule, or is this more difficult than it used to be? One of the biggest "myths" I run into is that NetWeaving is great for younger upwardly mobile types trying to establish new connections, but not so great for established executives, managers, and business owners who already have established networks. Nothing could be farther from the truth. Everyone enjoys making new connections, especially creative and successful people. Variety truly is the spice of life and meeting new people and establishing new connections and relationships is what keeps people young in mind and young at heart. Gerontologists have also discovered that maintaining an active life of "socialization" and "relationship building" is one of the key components in predicting longer life expectancy.

BECOMING A BETTER RESOURCE FOR OTHERS (A VIRTUAL SERGEANT BILKO, OR RADAR IN MASH)

- How can I help you? This is the simplest NetWeaving question and yet in many ways, it is the most powerful. For some of the best NetWeavers, this is the only question they routinely ask.

- What do you consider to be some of your most valuable information resources and sources you count on? This can not only open doors for new resources which you can add to your resource inventory, but may also introduce you to parties who can become part of your trusted resource network.

- Of the websites, books, and articles which you keep for reference, what are some of the ones you most rely on and why? This is similar to the above question, but it may bring out different responses.

- Of all of the great ideas you've heard over your life, or great mentors you've had, what would you say are the one or two most important ideas or lessons you've learned? Wow! This one will make you grow. Another way of asking something similar: What would you consider to be the secret of your success over the years in your business and your personal life?

ASSEMBLING A "TRUSTED RESOURCE NETWORK" (MADE UP OF "BEST OF BREED" IN A WIDE RANGE OF INDUSTRIES, PROFESSIONS, AND SPECIALTIES)—YOU ARE IN A RECRUITING MODE HERE AND YOU ARE IDENTIFYING AND "QUALIFYING" POTENTIAL RESOURCES

- What are some of the best ways you've seen or that you've practiced to provide "exceptional" service in your business, practice, or industry?

- In your opinion, which companies that you do business with do you most admire for providing exceptional service during and after a sale? How do you translate that into the way you run your business?

- Is there anyone who comes to mind who has a "trusted resource network" and whom you routinely call because you recognize this deep and qualified network they have at their disposal?

A JIGSAW PUZZLE REAL LIFE EXAMPLE

You are talking with a friend who confides that her job is insecure due to problems within the industry. Her income is below where she really wants it be in order to adequately contribute toward the family income. You ask a series of NetWeaving-type questions and are impressed with her answers.

Nevertheless, whether due to procrastination, fear of the unknown, a struggling economy and tight job market, she is resistant to make a move. You, who know, trust, and respect her abilities, learn about a job opening at a company where you know someone fairly high up.

You suggest she write a job description of what she would really like to be doing based upon her strengths, and you help by reading it and making suggestions. You see her strengths to be a good match with the skill sets required for the company concerned.

You go one step farther. You tell her about the opportunity, have her send you her resume, and send it on to the person you know within the company, along with a letter of recommendation of your own. Your contact gets her resume to the people conducting the search.

You also make an initial overture, testing the water by sounding your contact out with her background, and offering to act as a reference source. You might even *host* a meeting to introduce the parties.

Your friend lands the job and within two years becomes a senior vice president of the company. Pipe dream, you might say. Not so. I've known many real life stories very similar to this and there are NetWeavers out there doing this as you read.

LEARN THE JIGSAW PUZZLE ANALOGY

It never fails. Every time I make a presentation on NetWeaving and I give the jigsaw puzzle analogy, referring to each of us as *"walking, talking jigsaw puzzles with pieces missing,"* a smile appears on people's faces. It really is a great way to graphically illustrate what NetWeaving is all about—being on the lookout for another person's missing pieces while we're out there searching for our own.

So practice telling this story as a way of explaining what NetWeaving is all about. In no time, you will find that you're getting good at it.

And watch the smile come across a person's face each time you tell it.

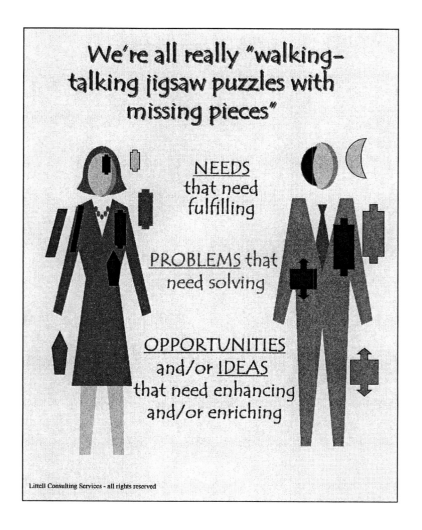

5

Learning To Listen And To Be Attuned With Two Pair Of Ears And Two Set Of Antennae— NetWeavers Learn To Listen

We have two ears and one mouth so that we can listen twice as much as we speak.
— Epictetus

In addition to the superficiality of traditional networking, the other main weakness is its *unilateral* focus on "*What's In It for ME?*" (WIIFMe). When most people are in a *networking* mode and mindset, they're tuning into conversations they're having on only one channel, and they're listening for the answer to only one question—"*Is this person a prospect or candidate for what I need or for what I have to offer?* or "*Can this person help me?*" And if the answer to that question is "*no*" or "*probably not*", a person in a networking mindset tunes the other person out, or just leaves, looking for greener pastures.

Don't get me wrong. We all need new business. We all need solutions to our own needs, problems, and opportunities and so there's nothing wrong with networking with our own needs *primarily* in mind.

But there's a different mindset when you're NetWeaving. The NetWeaver is listening with two pair of ears and is tuned in with two sets of antennae. With one, he or she is still listening for whether this person with whom they are talking is a potential prospect for what they have to offer or someone who can solve a problem, or fulfill a need they have. After all, as we've said over and over again, there's nothing wrong with traditional networking. But with the other set of ears or antennae, the NetWeaver is listening and trying to tune in for opportunities to help the other person find some of his or her *missing pieces.*

The three key questions which, persons can train themselves to ask in virtually every conversation—phone, email, or in person:

- Is there someone I know who would benefit from meeting or knowing this person?

- Are there resources which this person could provide to some of my friends, clients, or prospects, or are there some gratuitous resources I could provide to him or her?

- Has this person impressed me so much that I should consider adding her or him to my trusted *resource network*?

This is the *essence* of becoming a skilled power NetWeaver and a great way to enrich the level of the dialogue, which we'll discuss later.

You might be asking, *"How am I supposed to genuinely be listening to what the other person is saying, while at the same time, scanning my mental rolodex to come up with a suitable match to suggest for the answer to any of these three questions?"* Fortunately, it's much easier than you might think, and with time and with practice, it becomes second nature.

It's a little bit like when you do anything for the first time. It stretches your existing mental capacity. When you move into a new neighborhood, everything is foreign to you. You must concentrate on how to get home and which turns to make. If it's a complicated subdivision, you probably make a mistake a few times. Then, as you repeat the route over and over again, and as your senses begin to fill in the familiarity of the surroundings, you can literally put the return home drive on automatic pilot and concentrate on other things. The next thing you know, you're home. Some of us find we get some of our best ideas when we're doing something which requires our *attention*, but not our complete *concentration*. That is what is taught in transcendental meditation in order to allow the mind to reach a higher state of awareness.

You've heard the statement many times about what a small portion of our brains we actually utilize and this NetWeaving exercise can actually make us better at everything we do.

TRY IT. . .YOU'LL LIKE IT!

Now here's a test!

The next time you're having a conversation with someone, especially someone you know well, as you're talking, ask yourself the three questions and see how easy it is. And guess what? The more you do it, the better you will get at it.

And the more you can create a "mental picture" of learning to listen with two pair of ears and tuning in with two sets of antennae, the more you will build this into a daily habit.

LEARNING TO LISTEN IS ONLY HALF THE BATTLE—THE OTHER HALF IS RETENTION

I have found unless I take notes very shortly after hearing information, I will not retain it very long—often less than 24 hours. I certainly won't remember many of the important details. What I have also discovered is that I only need to write *key words* down as I am listening (or very shortly thereafter), rather than worrying about complete sentences. If I come back to my notes within the first 24 hours or less, I am surprised at how much I can retain. The key words trigger your brain to recall more of the specific details.

From this point on, don't collect a single business card without writing a couple of key words or a key fact on the back concerning your conversation.

This lesson about how quickly we forget and the importance

of followup is central to what we are learning from a project I am helping run at the Buckhead Club in Atlanta.

Bill Nordmark, a member of the club and a bright young man with wisdom far beyond his years, heard a talk I made on "NetWeaving" and volunteered to help form a group called "Eight at Eight" (putting eight members together at an 8:00 A.M. breakfast at the club to get to know each other better). I was invited to become part of the "Eight at Eight Council" made up of a small group of members who meet quarterly to assess the progress of the project. Each of the council members agrees to "host" (together with one other council member) two meetings each quarter. Kendall Craig, the event planner at the club, and Jeff Goldworn, the club manager, were totally supportive of the project. After only a few of these breakfast "table" meetings, prominently positioned by Kendall and Jeff where other members could see it, the events are now booked solid and have a long waiting list.

In addition to going around the table and introducing each of the persons—a little of their business and personal history, how they became involved in the club, and something about their family and their outside interests—we also encouraged them to answer some of the key questions we stress in NetWeaving: *What does a "best" prospect for you look like including some of your current clients? And what is your strategic advantage that differentiates you from others?*

But what truly has been the real "eye opener" for me was what happened when I volunteered at the first meeting to be the "scribe" and take notes. I then sent my rough notes out in e-mail form to each of the participants. I asked them to make corrections and add important points about themselves which they may have forgotten to mention or maybe didn't stress enough during the meeting. I asked them to return them to me so we could circulate to all who had been in attendance.

Several things struck me as I started getting these notes back. I *misheard* a number of points which the persons clarified, and perhaps more importantly, most thought of additional information which was as, if not more important and useful, than some of what was mentioned during the meeting.

We now are incorporating an outline for the two council member hosts to use as they are moderating the meeting with one of them agreeing to serve in this role as the scribe, and repeating the process of circulating the notes after they come back in edited form.

Also there is a "reunion party" scheduled. Everyone in attendance will be given a copy of the notes on all of the other participants in each of the groups, put into a booklet form. This has been the most successful of all the NetWeaving experiments which we've tried to date, and the notetaking and the followup have been one of the keys.

Learning to be a great NetWeaver first involves the skill sets of NetWeaving—being a connector of others as well as a gratuitous resource provider. But unless you are willing to admit our brains need all the help we can give them—therefore necessitating that we take notes within a fairly short time period after meeting someone in a "how can I help you?" context—you will never reach your full NetWeaving potential.

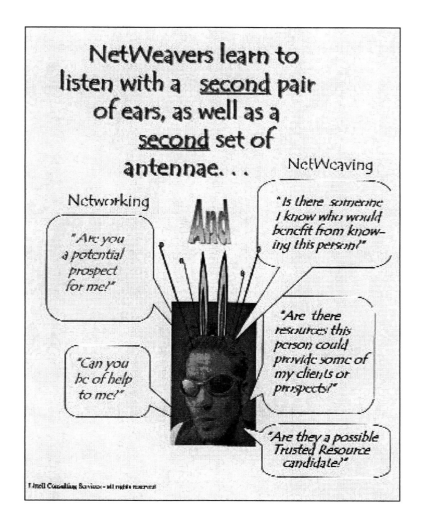

6

How To Build Relationships And Establish Trust—How Relationships Are Formed

Trust dies but mistrust blossoms.
— SOPHOCLES

The more I've worked with the concept of NetWeaving and have observed the positive effects it can have on business and personal lives, the more convinced I've become that NetWeaving can actually have some positive impact on our entire world. This has become especially evident since 9/11. We as a country, and as an international community, must pull together more on a daily basis, rather than just as a reaction to the next tragic event which occurs because, in this terrorist world we now live in, trouble is almost certainly going to be occurring on a more regular basis.

I'm equally convinced that we aren't going to stay together and help each other purely out of altruism.

In an idealistic world, everyone would be looking out for everyone else's interests in addition to their own. Realistically, we look out for our own interests first, and we tend to pay lip service to our altruism in looking out for others' interests as well. We shouldn't beat ourselves up too badly for this. It's just the darker side of human nature and something most of us try to improve upon over our lifetimes.

What if it could become almost universally accepted that by NetWeaving—genuinely putting others' needs, problems, and opportunities on a more equal plane with our own— and within the scope of universal laws of reciprocity, consistent with almost all religions and belief systems—that NetWeaving could become a "self-serving" universal form of currency, whose deposits plus interest will accumulate and someday will mature and endow?

Of course, one of the dangers is similar to the invention of nuclear fusion. Although it can either be used to supply a nerer-ending supply of energy to the world, in the wrong hands, it can become our worst nightmare and the roots of disaster. I don't worry whether or not this could happen with NetWeaving. It will happen. Charlatans have been around since one caveman tried to convince another that a "square" stone wheel would actually work better than a "round" one.

There will be pretenders (especially as the concept continues to grow in popularity and visibility) and others who will mask themselves as NetWeavers and as NetWeaving ambassadors, but who in fact are using the word and the concept as a way to artificially paint themselves in an altruistic light. As in everyday life, we must learn to celebrate genuine NetWeavers and when recognized, disassociate ourselves from "false NetWeavers."

Admittedly, this will be easier said than done. Proven legitimacy, credibility, and consistency over time are the only real judges. The best way to guard against "NetWeaving" false prophets is to watch the way these potential NetWeavers live their daily lives and look at how they treat people. Forget about what they say: look at what they do and what others say about them.

TRUST-BUILDING AS A SALES APPROACH

Many books have been written on relationship-building as a sales technique. No judgmental statement is typically made about whether getting people to buy something or hire or contract with someone for services rendered by creating a sense of trust is good or bad. With many sales systems, establishing trust is seen as a means to an end—the avenue to success—and the ethical considerations are omitted.

Creating trust, using a variety of methods and techniques but with your own interests in mind, is not necessarily bad or deceitful. I've just learned that relationship-building in a NetWeaving context eliminates most if not all of the negative aspects and ethical conflicts. At the same time, it creates results in the long run which tend to be as good or better than those from the more "what's in it for me" sales and marketing approaches.

THE RELATIONSHIP-BUILDING PROCESS— THE PINNACLE IS TRUST

You've heard when we first meet someone, we make judgments

and assessments about the person, based primarily on her or his physical appearance: dress, mannerisms, as well as things which we don't fully understand. Whether you want to call it "chemistry or body language" or just "vibes", there are some people who have a natural advantage in looks, appearance, charisma, or some other form of radiated charm and appeal which touches the other person.

A few years ago, as a former chairman of a national organization, I was invited to a past chairman's breakfast at which our keynote speaker for that annual meeting was going to be present. At each of the tables set for eight persons, there was one chair left vacant. When our speaker came into the room, he went around and spent about 10 to 15 minutes at each table.

The speaker was Colin Powell, former Armed Forces Chief of Staff, and now Secretary of State. He hadn't been seated and started speaking for more than a few minutes before you felt as if you'd known him your entire life. He just had an aura and presence about him which almost immediately made you want to like and trust him.

Call it charisma, presence, demeanor, or whatever; maybe it's genetic or at least partly so, there are some people who just start out with an advantage on the relationship and trust-building side over the rest of us.

Hopefully with constructive input from others, whether it's learning how to dress appropriately, or how to eliminate some of these "blind spots" which others can see, we can avoid some of the most obvious things which turn other people off. But in most cases, relationship-building starts when someone opens his or her mouth.

Every so often, a new idea or new concept comes along which is so simple and so universally accepted, that it takes off. I feel fortunate that this is what's happening with NetWeaving and I think I know why.

IT'S ALL ABOUT RELATIONSHIPS, STUPID!

As I analyzed the process of NetWeaving more and more, and studied and interviewed those people whom I or others identified as "natural NetWeavers", I began to develop a new view of how relationships are formed and nurtured.

The pinnacle of all relationship-building is "trust" and yet trust isn't established overnight. As previously stated, I do believe some people have a built-in advantage in building trust, sometimes almost instantaneously.

Nevertheless, there's hope for the rest of us as well. NetWeaving can play a critical role in helping each person get much better at establishing relationships, and eventually building and maintaining trust.

HOW DO YOU BUILD RELATIONSHIPS AND ESTABLISH TRUST?

All relationships start with verbal *communication*. Sure, there are physical attributes and signs sent back and forth. These sometimes cause us to make snap judgments based soley on appearance, body language, and perceived chemistry or lack of it, but by and large, relationships begin or end when people begin a dialogue.

Almost all dialogue begins with some form of small talk. Most of us need *small talk* to overcome the awkwardness that we feel when we meet someone new, especially if it's one-on-one or within a very small group.

The biggest single problem with most traditional networking which goes on at business networking events, or just in social or business gatherings, is that the conversations tend to stay at the superficial level and never really progress beyond that. Sure, maybe there is a brief discussion of, "*What's your line of work?*" and maybe some talk about the industry, or your job in particular, but the point is little conversation takes place which actually helps establish or nurture any kind of a "growth" relationship.

IT TAKES INITIATIVE AND COURAGE TO MOVE TO A MEANINGFUL DIALOGUE!

When I first was analyzing the relationship-building process in my mind, I came up with the word "initiative" to describe the way that in midst of this awkward, superficial stage, someone lifts the level of conversation and moves it to what I refer to as *meaningful dialogue.*

Following one of my NetWeaving presentations, during which I explained this step in the process, Pat Haley, president of National Personnel Recruiters and a great NetWeaver, suggested I add the word, *courage* alongside of *initiative*. After all, almost all of us feel somewhat awkward during this *small talk* stage. Someone who can elevate the discussion to "meaningful dialogue" is exhibiting *courage* since there's always the chance that no one else will follow their lead and begin contributing at that higher level.

It is at this stage that the value of NetWeaving really becomes key in helping facilitate and speed up the relationship-building process. Since NetWeaving is all about helping others—connecting people with other people, and providing others with the information and resources they need—focusing on the problems and the needs of others not only promotes meaningful conversation, but it leads those listening to want to do the same.

It's similar to what happens in a traffic jam when cars aren't moving and someone is courteous and lets someone in from a side street who's been waiting for some time. Look back in your rear view mirrors and others will start doing the same thing, once someone takes the first initiative. It's the same with NetWeaving. It's contagious! The more people who do it, the more who will want to do it.

YOU CONNECT OR DECIDE TO DISCONNECT

Simply having a meaningful dialogue does not necessarily mean you're going to *connect* with everyone in the discussion. In fact, based upon a person's attitudes or responses, you may make the decisions to *disconnect*, meaning you really don't care if you *ever* see that person again. But keep in mind—we all have our bad moments. Sometimes giving someone a second chance in a different context and under a different set of circumstances may let you see him or her in an entirely new light and change your attitude completely.

If you are involved in a conversation, and if you are the one who shows the initiative and courage to shift the dialogue toward helping others, you are in most cases *enhancing your own image* as you focus on their needs and problems. This may just be one of the best and fastest ways to help other people decide that they would like to connect with you, so long as the help offered is genuine and without a hidden agenda.

CONNECTING WITH OTHERS RAISES THE LEVEL OF APPRECIATION AND PROMOTES ACCEPTANCE

As other people observe you shifting the conversation to them or to others in the group, you subconsciously raise their level of appreciation for you. You are not only solidifying the connection you make, you increase the chances of gaining their "acceptance."

ENRICH THE EXPERIENCE

Another step in relationship-building which raises the level of appreciation and increases the chances of acceptance is by "enriching" the experience.

A few years ago, a good friend of mine passed away but I'll always remember one day we spent together. Jim and I began our careers in the life insurance business in Denver, Colorado, at about the same time. We were so poor back then that we used to take turns going down five flights of stairs from the small office we shared to put coins in the parking meter to avoid parking lot rates.

We both loved the outdoors and loved to hike. On one such hiking trip in the Colorado Rockies, we went up what would best be described as a chimney. It was a narrow opening that you had to crawl up either with your hands and feet, and at some points with just your back against one wall and your feet on the other wall to short of shimmy up. We could tell how high we were going because we could see light up at the top.

After several hours of exhaustive work, we climbed out into what might best be described as a scene right out of the Sound of Music, (you know the scene, "The Hills are Alive. . .") a late spring day, beautiful blue sky, breeze blowing across our sweaty bodies, wild flowers everywhere you looked, pure mountain air mixed in with nature's fragrances. Still today, I can literally close my eyes wherever I am, and instantaneously be right there. It had a profound impact on almost all my senses—sight, feeling/touch, sound, and smell. If I'd have eaten a dandelion, I'd have experienced every sense.

Amy K. Hutchens, the authority on brain research mentioned earlier, tells us that the more senses you touch, the better our recollection of the event or meeting will be.

Also, Amy K. tells us that her research shows that what people most recall from a meeting is not necessarily what you said or not even necessarily what you looked like.

What they are most likely to retain will be the *experience*— how you made them feel—about you, but even more importantly, how you made them feel about themselves. When you do either or both of these, you are *enriching the experience.*

That's another reason why both doing NetWeaving, as well as spreading the word about NetWeaving and inspiring others to do the same, helps increase the chances people will remember you in a positive way. Not only did you connect them or offer to connect them with others or provide resources they needed, but you also exposed them to a concept which was inspirational and aspirational in nature. You made them richer by learning about it. Once again, you enriched the experience.

THE PINNACLE OF RELATIONSHIP— BUILDING IS TRUST

It would be unusual if this entire process would take place during one conversation or one encounter, but it can and does happen, especially if you the NetWeaver are facilitating the process. In most cases, somewhere along the way, the person involved in the conversation decides they like what they hear; they *connect* with what you're doing and saying, they gain an *appreciation* for the quality of the person they've seen in action; then they *bond* with you.

Even if it takes a second meeting (or longer) to truly establish trust, the basis for all lasting relationships, has begun.

TRUST ERODES WITHOUT FOLLOWTHROUGH AND FOLLOWUP

Once trust is established, it doesn't mean it's there for good. All relationships need healthy doses of reinforcement and encouragement. In the absence of follow-through and followup, what was originally viewed as "trust" may change to feelings that the person was really insincere and not genuine, and that their trust in the person was misplaced. Then the trust begins to erode. Following up simply means staying in contact and continuing to look for ways to be of help. The best way to do this is to continue connecting people with other people and to provide them with additional information and resources.

CONCLUSION—A KEY FOR ALL INDUSTRIES

Learning more about NetWeaving will hopefully inspire more industries to dedicate themselves to getting back to the basics of genuine relationship-building. By helping other people without an *immediate* concern for how they might personally benefit up front, many of the problems within the business world and society in general would disappear or become less serious.

Not everyone will buy into NetWeaving. They don't need

to. Only a small percentage of the population needs to do it in order to have a dramatic impact on everyone. That's because it truly is contagious and with a strong core of people doing it, it will become the thing to do, and a way by which people will be inspired to live their lives and run their businesses.

A FUN STORY OF NETWEAVING AND RELATIONSHIP BUILDING

Last year, my wife and I took what had to have been one of the greatest trips we've ever done—heli-hiking in the Canadian Rockies. Canadian Mountain Holidays owns three lodges in the Bugaboos and initially just was using them during the winter for Heli-Skiing for which they are booked solid year after year. Ski enthusiasts like to ski where there are no one else's tracks and except for the few persons in their party, almost no other skiers. They found they needed to keep the lodges open year-round, so they began attracting hikers. They pick you up in the morning, pack a lunch for you, and the helicopter takes you from base camp up to 8,000 to 9,000 feet where you start hiking. It might have taken you all day hiking to get to this point where you already have spectacular views.

On the bus ride up, there happened to be one gregarious character who stood out from the others. Although we didn't realize it at the time, we were beginning a relationship whose journey is only now just beginning.

As we learned, Alex Tilley and his friend Lynda were there

for more than just the scenery and adventure. If you have ever heard of a Tilley hat, you already know who Alex Tilley is. He invented a broad-brimmed canvas hat which has both a chin-strap as well as another strap which fits snugly at the back of your neck so that the hat will not blow off. I ran into a friend at the Buckhead Business Association who had just passed the hat he had owned for many years (guaranteed for life) down to his son as a rite of passage.

Alex, founder and chairman of Tilley Endurables, Inc., was there taking photos which would be appearing in his next cata-logue which, we now have.

I have been around NetWeavers long enough to spot a "natural one" when I see one and I could tell Alex had been NetWeaving all his life and this explained much of the reason for his success.

My wife and I have recently returned from a trip to Toronto to visit Alex and several of his friends. Other than the fact it was -10 degrees with a wind chill factor of about -30 degrees we had a fabulous time. I asked Alex to give me a NetWeaving story, and here's a great one.

A couple years ago at Rotary, Alex sat beside Jack Parker, now 86, and spoke to him of the challenges he was having man-aging his growing business. Jack told Alex that at age 31, he had been the world-wide president of Thermos, and since then had managed many companies. He also told Alex that he was bored.

"Why not come and give us a hand," Alex asked. *"Love to, and I'll work for free! See you Monday!"* he replied.

Jack, who Alex says, *"is the smartest of all of us when he's here at our world headquarters,*" shows up early three days a week, sits in on meetings and gives Alex and his company a lot of solid guidance.

Alex counseled, "*We're becoming world famous in certain parts of Canada so I'm often asked by young entrepreneurs for suggestions on getting started. I usually turn them over to Jack, who, with his vast experience, listens carefully, then gives them helpful criticism leavened with encouragement.*"

Jack benefits through the joy he receives from giving, and the recipients of his wisdom stand a much better chance at succeeding than they would have. "*She was going to lose her shirt!*" was one of Jack's comments to Alex about a young woman's business plans. "*Because of what he advised me, I'm redoing all my projections,*" she later told Alex.

Alex says, "*It's heart-warming to be of service to others, isn't it?*"

Approach every potential connection you make with an open mind and with the thought that this next person(s) may become a life-long friend(s) and someone who can help you grow in new ways you never experienced before. Hopefully the reverse will be true in what I can bring to their table. That's NetWeaving in a personal sense but it's also one of the real joys of life—creating new healthy and meaningful human relationships.

7

Why Don't More People NetWeave, And Why Don't People NetWeave More Often

All right everyone, line up alphabetically according to your height.
— CASEY STENGEL

NETWEAVING ISN'T RIGHT FOR EVERYONE

If NetWeaving is so "win-win-win-win" how come more people don't NetWeave, and why don't those who do *some* of it, do more of it?

First, although I hate to admit it, there are some people who I don't believe will EVER get it. It may be that they're just too much about "*what's in it for me?*", or they may be so "short-term" in their thinking that they don't want to allocate any of their time to something which doesn't seem to have a guarantee of an *immediate* pay-off (which NetWeaving actually does but they miss it). And what's really sad is they'll also miss some of the very *biggest* payoffs which come over time—only after strong relationships are built. The benefits to NetWeaving—back and forth—are often cumulative.

WATCH OUT HANGING AROUND WITH THOSE WHO JUST WON'T GET IT

Unfortunately some well-intentioned NetWeavers fall into a trap of NetWeaving with and for people who just aren't into *giving*. The fact that the NetWeaver gives, and yet nothing is coming back, just makes him or her want to try that much harder. At some point, after the NetWeaver has given and given, and seen nothing coming back, he or she either needs to accept the fact the person for whom they've been NetWeaving isn't and probably will never be a *giver*. They just need to move on, or vocalize their feelings to the person. In some cases this can have a profound impact, but in my experience, in most cases, *"what you see is what you get."*

There's an admonition in the Elton John/Tim Rice song "Circle of Life" which is very appropriate in understanding one of the key aspects of NetWeaving: *"Don't take more than you give."*

In life you find that there are givers and there are takers, and then there are all shades in between. Natural NetWeavers are heavy on the giving side because they find that the more they give, the more they seem to get in return. They do their NetWeaving, without thought for how or whether or not they're going to benefit in return. They just believe in the law of reciprocity.

On the other hand there are those who either are way over on the taking side, or when they give, it's **almost always** with an obvious or implied string attached.

Those who are takers never really learn to listen with a

second pair of ears because they're too focused on how they can benefit personally.

And unfortunately, some people are very good at being disguised NetWeavers. They talk the talk, but don't *walk the walk.* Sometimes the only way you know is that you just keep giving, but you don't see anything coming in return. When this becomes apparent, you need to just move on.

BUT FOR PEOPLE WHO WANT TO HELP OTHER PEOPLE

What about those people who genuinely like helping other people; and who may already be doing some NetWeaving, but who could be doing much more?

First, if people aren't aware of the basics of NetWeaving, they won't even realize when they're doing it. Since they don't recognize NetWeaving, even when they're doing it, they don't do it on a daily basis. When they begin to understand that there are skill sets which, with practice, can be substantially improved, they become more effective with their NetWeaving and they start doing it more often.

I saw a great example of this as I was kicking off a "user's group" meeting for Xerox with the NetWeaving theme. I not only saw how well this concept was received but I saw how it got the various parties (in some ways, competitors) attending the meeting to be more sharing and open—understanding that by helping others, they were in turn being helped. Another reason why the NetWeaving message had a major impact was the way the persons handling the meeting reinforced the word, and openly promoted the concept throughout the two-day meeting.

A SPECIAL CASE WITH ATTORNEYS AND CPAS

Of all professions, attorneys and CPAs are most ideally positioned to be NetWeavers for their clients. CPAs particularly, because of their need to have knowledge of the total client's tax picture, typically know more about their clients than any of the other professionals. Studies also show that of all the advisors, CPAs tend to have the highest level of trust. Yet few attorneys and even fewer CPAs do much if any strategic "matchmaking"—offering to put some of their clients together to find ways that they could be of help to each other.

In both cases, most attorneys and CPAs have an overriding fear that if they were to connect two of their clients, and something were not to work out as planned, they would somehow be held responsible.

Yet they take risks every day in their practices—accountants and attorneys in giving tax and legal advice, as well as attorneys in drafting legal documents. When they begin to understand that NetWeaving just involves taking a different kind of risk than they are used to assuming, they can begin to change.

NetWeaving simply involves *relationship* risk. Yes, there is risk. But by passing up the "golden opportunity" to connect some of their clients or to ask them if introducing them to some of their other clients would be something they would see as being of value, they miss all the positive outcomes which could be forthcoming to their clients and back to themselves.

One of the best ways for CPAs and attorneys to play the matchmaking role is to put on a client appreciation event (a breakfast, lunch or dinner) where "advance" information about NetWeaving is sent out as part of the invitation. This way, they understand that the idea is to look for ways they might be able to help others who will be attending to:

- make new connections and provide contacts the other person might find valuable

- provide resources (in addition to their own) which would be of value, etc.

CEO groups are also beginning to catch on to NetWeaving. To some extent, when YPO (Young President's Organization—for persons who had become presidents of their company before age 44) was formed, they were all about NetWeaving without calling it that.

One CEO group in Dallas, Texas, formed by John Casey with help initially from Mark Schooler, was actually founded with NetWeaving in mind. They asked for permission to use the name "the NetWeavers" since their mission is to consistently look for ways to help each other by connecting members with the people and resources which will make them better at what they do. What started out mostly as NetWeaving has nurtured many strong new friendships and relationships, both business and personal.

It's long been a mistaken belief that CEOs have all the contacts they could possibly want. That may be true in some isolated cases but groups such as YPO (Young President's Organization) and WPO, as well as TEC (The Executive Committee), and several others have demonstrated the value of forming strong relationships with other CEOs who can act as a sounding board and can become a great way to expand their resource base.

People pay tens or hundreds of thousands of dollars to join exclusive country clubs. At least part of the reason they do is *access to power*, figuring that people with the money to join will be influential contacts for business and social purposes.

NetWeaving can do the same thing—just without the high entry fee. Your dues are paid by helping connect other people and by sharing your talents and your resources with others. As you become known as a resource, you develop the reputation for being an American fish—a USA CARP—a "Universally Sought-After Connector And Resource Provider").

THOSE WHO SAY THEY'VE DONE A LOT BUT NOT MUCH HAS COME BACK AROUND

I have to put those who have told me something along these lines into two distinct groups.

The first group is mostly composed of persons who think

they're NetWeaving but they're not. It is obvious to everyone (other than themselves) that, by their actions, words, or some combination thereof, they're connecting people or providing resources to someone else, with an understanding that they are expecting something in return . . . the old *"I'll scratch your back, but only if you agree to scratch mine."*

When this is done, guess what, the other party doesn't see it as NetWeaving and therefore doesn't feel any real obligation to return the favor. In some cases, they are actually turned off by the approach, which they see as a form of disguised self-interest.

But there is a second group from whom I heard this same point about not seeing much of their NetWeaving coming back around, and yet I believe their motives were pure, or mostly pure. As I studied this in more detail, something became very clear.

THE NUMBER ONE REASON PEOPLE DON'T BENEFIT FROM THEIR NETWEAVING—LACK OF FOLLOW UP AND FOLLOW THROUGH

Take this as a simple example. You and I meet at a chamber of commerce meeting where NetWeaving has become a recognized way of life.

As I am asking you for ways which I can help you and you tell me about someone who I saw earlier and who I know is at the meeting. I survey the room; see the person and bring her over to make an introduction. After a short but meaningful discussion, I suggest we look at calendars and set up a meeting that I can host for the two persons.

The meeting takes place and the two people really hit it off and end up discussing a number of ways which they can help each other.

Everything sounds great, and we find time and time again, at the end of the meeting, one or both of the persons who have been connected, ask the NetWeaver host, how they might be able to help him or her.

This whole scenario sounds like a grand slam home run for everyone involved. It looks as if everyone is going to be helped. There's only one problem.

All of us are so busy these days and "time-stressed" that within a week, if no follow-up action is taken, chances are that all of the positive things discussed, and all of the potential connections which could be made or resources provided, will be lost in the cosmic dust of lost and faded memories.

A serious NetWeaver host should take one additional step as the host and send a follow up e-mail or letter to each of the two persons summarizing what each said he or she was going to do. Then in a couple weeks, he or she should follow up to see if either or both of the parties have followed through.

This is what separates the great NetWeavers from the "dabblers," and what separates amateur NetWeavers from those who will make a difference in the world with their NetWeaving activities and actions.

ONE MORE PROBLEM—THE NETWEAVING TREE OF MULTIPLE CONNNECTIONS

Not only does the NetWeaving which we do lose much of its potential when we don't follow up. Someting worse happens. The number one reason much of our NetWeaving doesn't come back to benefit us is that *connections* that we and others make fall victim to our short-lived memories.

One clear and embarrassing example of this occurred when I was asked to speak on a panel at the North Fulton Chamber of Commerce. I have since forgotten the name of the person who asked me to speak at the meeting at which I met Jack Pilger, Jim Cichanski, and Marty Friedman, all great NetWeavers, and persons with whom I continue to work with to this day.

This happened to me and I'm supposed to be pretty good at this stuff. We often forget who made a connection for our benefit! We forget who provided us with which resource!

Unless the person, who **made** the connection, or who **provided** the resource, comes back at some point in time (pretty soon after the connection is made) and asks the person they initially helped how things worked out, their NetWeaving often goes unrecognized and unrewarded. It's not that we aren't grateful, we just plain forget. As we build the relationship, we tend to undervalue the fact that, had the person not made the original connection, none of this would have taken place.

When a person commits to becoming a skilled NetWeaver, he/she will find him/herself consistently challenged to keep track of all the *missing pieces* to another person's jigsaw puzzles that they're attempting to solve.

Although we now have designed software to automate this process, you will find a form in the appendix of this book which will help you build NetWeaving into your daily habits.

SOME WILL JUST NEVER BE GOOD MATCHMAKERS—THEY CAN STILL LEARN TO POSITION THEMSELVES BETTER AS RESOURCE PROVIDERS

Those who are just too shy, or too introverted to ever see themselves as "matchmakers," can nevertheless still become great NetWeavers by becoming skilled at *positioning* themselves as a *resource* to others and especially by building and expanding their Trusted Resource Network.

THE TOP TEN REASONS PEOPLE DON'T NETWEAVE AT ALL OR NETWEAVE MORE

10. They aren't aware of the skill sets and therefore don't recognize when they're NetWeaving.

9. They have never thought of NetWeaving as something with learnable skills which most can master.

8. People forget. As with any new skill which people begin learning, unless they build it into their daily habits, they will soon forget to do it on a regular basis.

7. They are too short-term in their thinking and view NetWeaving as something with too long-term a payoff to dedicate any real time towards.

6. Some persons are very analytical by nature and have a problem being perceived as nosey and would prefer to be viewed as helpful problem-solvers.

5. Some analyticals feel uncomfortable in a "matchmaking" role but could still excel in the "resource-providing" aspects of NetWeaving.

4. Some people, especially CPAs and attorneys have an over-riding fear of connecting some of their clients, for fear that it might not work out and that it could reflect negatively (or worse) back on them for making the introduction.

3. Some are just too all about "what's in it for me." It's generally a losing battle to try and convert someone who falls into this category.

2. They give up NetWeaving at some point because they don't think they see anything coming back.

1. People carry NetWeaving up to a certain point but then fail to follow through or follow up and the results fall short of their potential.

8

MATCHMAKING IN ACTION—
REFERRALS AND HOSTING—
WHY IS HOSTING DIFFERENT?

*There's a magic chemistry created when good people
bring other good people together. . .and no two formulae are alike.*
— R. S. LITTELL

Imagine you are attending just about any business networking
meeting you are used to. You are in conversation with Darlene,
someone whom you just met and who has been asking you a
number of fairly in-depth questions about your business and
your needs. It surprises you how open you are being with your
answers. It's partly because she prefaced her questions with a little explanation of a new word she's learned describing something she thinks she's been doing most of her life—just without
a good word for it. She calls it "NetWeaving," a golden rule
form of networking which is all about putting the other person's
needs, problems, or opportunities first, or at least at a somewhat
comparable level to your own. Also, the way she's asking the
questions supports your belief that she's not doing it just for her
own benefit. She's genuinely interested in finding ways to help.

You are subsequently very impressed by how helpful she is

in suggesting various persons to whom she will introduce you, and/or gratuitous resources with which she might be able to provide you or to which she could refer you.

Suddenly out of the corner of her eye, Darlene spots someone she recognizes and before you know it, you are being almost dragged halfway across the room and introduced to Tom, obviously an acquaintance of Darlene's. After Darlene and Tom have a warm, short catch-up conversation, Darlene begins rattling off things about you and your business and Tom's, and why she believes there might be some room for collaboration and/or ways you could help each other.

You have just been in the presence of a "Master NetWeaver." Here a few giveaway signs of a master NetWeaver:

- A person who comes across as genuinely interested in other people's needs, problems, and opportunities.

- Someone with a seemingly insatiable desire to connect people for their benefit—to solve problems and fulfill needs and opportunities they have—some which they don't even recognize.

- An individual who, as you get to know him or her, just seems to be a walking, talking rolodex of contacts, resources, and information.

- And the next day or within a couple of days, you get a follow up e-mail, telephone call or letter from the person, following through with several of the things you discussed and people with whom the person was going to connect you.

HOW DID THESE NATURAL NETWEAVERS GET THIS WAY?

Some people just seem to be naturally gregarious and float effortlessly about during social and business situations meeting and greeting new people as if they'd known them all their life. With some, it's because they just genuinely enjoy making these connections because it just makes them feel good.

Others do it partly because they enjoy it and partly because they have found it to be an interesting way to help them overcome some of their own feelings of insecurity in social situations.

Take the case of the plain Jane, the "wallflower" who goes out on the town with her good-looking but very shy friend, Suzie. Plain Jane finds by being outgoing and initiating conversations, she is helping her friend make contacts and friends, as well as making contacts herself which she wouldn't have made on her own. Is this "using" the other person?

Most of us are still trying to figure out how to get along with each other. In my opinion, almost any means that isn't destructive and overly manipulative, and which helps us break out of our typical routine in order to establish more new healthy human relationships should be welcomed.

But for some of us, especially persons who tend to be more

on the shy or analytical side, this meeting and greeting new people and establishing relationships is often challenging and even threatening.

Psychologists say the number one fear is not fear of heights or even snakes or spiders. It's fear of public speaking. And a large part of this is the fear of being rejected, or embarrassing oneself in front of a group of people. From speaking to large groups, this fear can easily extend to meeting persons in smaller groups or even one-on-one. To some highly analytical and shy persons, meeting new people and establishing relationships translates into a mini-version of this fear of public speaking. Many analyticals much prefer to be viewed as helpful—behind-the-scenes problem-solvers.

We have discovered something very interesting about NetWeaving. Because it's all about helping connect people for their benefit and not our own, many more analytical types who were uncomfortable or downright nervous in this meeting-other-people capacity have found that they actually enjoy NetWeaving connections they make and can get quite good at it.

Realistically, though, there are some shyer persons who still will not feel comfortable in this matchmaking role and they should concentrate their energies on improving their skills as a strategic resource provider and on learning how better to position themselves as such with others.

But what about those who are already good at NetWeaving? They will probably be the ones who will benefit the most. Much of the secret to NetWeaving simply involves raising one's awareness, learning how to build NetWeaving skill sets into your daily habits, as well as how to spread the word to others about this "win-win-win-win" form of networking.

DOING IT SIMPLY BECAUSE YOU ENJOY IT

Even if you've never done much matchmaking before, most people find they enjoy it for several reasons:

- They genuinely enjoy helping other people. Most people have never really thought of all the benefits that come from connecting other people. But the more they do it, the more they want to do.

- There's a "rush" that comes from connecting two people and watching the energy that they create as they find ways to help each other; people they discover they know in common, and so on and so on.

- The NetWeaver experiences the "halo" effect. They feel their own image enhanced and elevated as the two persons connected now see them in a much different and more generous light.

DOING IT—WITH AND WITHOUT KEEPING SCORE

We said this earlier, but it bears repeating. One of the negative comments I hear time and time again about persons who join "leads" groups is they hate the feeling that everyone is "keeping score," whether they come out and say it or not *("Ok, I gave you a lead, you now owe me one")*. With NetWeaving , no one keeps score. You give and you give and at some point, as you give and you see nothing coming back in return, you simply assume (until proven to the contrary) this person is a taker and not a giver. You just go on. As you get more skilled in your NetWeaving, you will be able to recognize this type of person sooner and avoid some of the frustrations.

THE FIRST STEP TOWARD BECOMING A BETTER NETWEAVING MATCHMAKER

As we mentioned in Chapter Five, the key to becoming a skilled NetWeaving matchmaker is to learn to listen differently—to create the habit of listening with a second pair of ears and to be tuned into conversations with a second set of antennae.

Here's how you can build this into a daily habit so that you will constantly be looking for opportunities to do this.

REFERRALS

When you ordinarily hear the word "referrals", especially in a sales or marketing context, you tend to think of it in terms of someone *referring a person to you*. Whether they are willing to admit it or not, a universal wish of all salesmen and saleswomen is, *"I'd much rather work referrals than cold calls."* I would much prefer if persons recommended me to others and referred business to me than for me to have to pick up the phone and call strangers or approach someone simply on a walk-in basis and introduce myself.

NetWeaving is the best way to get referrals, but it's because it's all about *making referrals to others.* The referrals come . . . to you . . . as an indirect effect of helping others. You don't ask for them; they just come.

NetWeaving changes your radar. Applying the idea of learning to listen and tuning in differently, imagine on most phone calls you make and in most conversations in which you are engaged, that you start redirecting your ears and your radar antennae.

You still will be listening for signals that this person may be able to help you with some of your own needs. There's nothing wrong with this. But with your newly installed radar, you're going to be listening and tuned in with these additional questions in mind:

- *Is there someone I know who would benefit from knowing this person, either personally or professionally?*

- *Could this person provide information or resources which would benefit someone I know?*

- *Has this person impressed me so much that I should consider getting to know him or her better, and possibly later, adding him or her to my Trusted Resource Network?*

You should also know that as you are asking yourself these three questions, whether it's on the telephone or in person, you need not be overly concerned with making a "perfect" strategic match with someone else. If you find this person interesting, creative, successful, funny, or just someone you've enjoyed meeting or talking with, chances are that others will feel the same way. That's half the fun of it. You just never know.

NETWEAVING REFERRALS AND HOSTING MEETINGS FOR CLIENTS AND PROSPECTIVE CLIENTS OF CPAS AND ATTORNEYS

Most attorneys and CPAs are sitting on a NetWeaving "goldmine" of "referral" connections they could be making, especially those specializing in the small business arena where many of their clients and prospective clients are small business entrepreneurs trying to get established or wishing to move their business to the next level. Stimulating introductions between and among clients and prospective clients—actually being an active *matchmaker*, is something that only a few do on any sort of a regular basis and yet it's one of the most valuable services they could provide.

As mentioned before, the primary reasons why some

attorneys don't do any of it include:

- "I'm concerned that I would connect two of my clients and something bad would happen and they would blame me or hold me responsible for having made the initial connection."

Although there is always the chance this could happen, those who don't NetWeave based upon a fear of "relationship risk" are missing (as are their clients) all the positive benefits that come from successful connections (business collaboration, referrals to other businesses or suppliers, new approaches to existing problems, friendships resulting from finding areas of commonality, etc., etc.).

- "I don't think it's professional for me to actively suggest or arrange connections with or among my clients and prospective clients."

Thank goodness some of the best and most successful attorneys not only disagree with this statement, but feel just the opposite. Connecting others, and acting as a gratuitous resource for others, not only is in line with rules of professional conduct, but it is *"servant leadership."* Putting the needs, problems, and opportunities of others first, not only pays off in the long run, but it is *contagious*. The more people do it and see others doing the same, the more others start doing it as well.

"PAY IT FORWARD" VERSION OF NETWEAVING

The Warner Bros. movie *"Pay It Forward"* is based upon a book by the same name written by Catherine Ryan Hyde (Simon & Schuster—publisher). In both the book and the movie, a seventh grade school teacher assigns his class a year-long project to create something which will change the world, and put it into action.

One of the seventh graders in the class, comes up with something very special. Up on the blackboard, he draws out a diagram of his concept of pay it forward. When someone does a "favor" for you, instead of paying him or her back, you pay it forward by doing a gratuitous act of kindness for three other people, and they in turn are obligated to do the same for three others, etc., etc., and it becomes an *exponential favor factory* with persons constantly looking for ways to do favors for others to repay favors done for them.

Sure, maybe it's a little on the idealistic side but there's nothing wrong with imagining that the world could be like that some day. I believe it would fit very well with Junior Achievement. (JA)

We hope to promote the Pay It Forward Foundation both within JA and elsewhere because we believe the two are closely aligned in their mission to help children develop an understanding that by helping others, you are also helping yourself. The Pay It Forward Foundation is bringing the pay it forward concept into the classrooms and inspiring children to learn early in life, that *"the more you give, the more you get in return."*

In addition, the pay it forward concept was what inspired

me to come up with what I believe makes a great business version which we refer to as PIONTTO. <u>P</u>ass <u>I</u>t <u>ON</u> <u>T</u>o <u>T</u>wo <u>O</u>thers (see page 87). Not only could it work very well in a business context, it is in fact already working because we have put it into action.

REFERRALS AND HOSTING

When we hear the word referral, especially if we're in any sales and marketing capacity, we tend to think of it in the WIIFMe context (i.e. "*I love having business referred to me.*") In a NetWeaving context, you must change your entire mindset. A referral means you are connecting two or more other people, and once again just doing it because you believe:

- They would benefit from meeting each other.

- They have things in common which lead you to believe there might be something synergistic in their meeting.

- They are both high quality people and good things happen when good people meet and figure ways to make good things happen.

We have created three Levels of referrals. You should think of these in conjunction with the analogy we covered earlier of learning to listen with a second pair of ears and a second set of antennae.

LEVEL 1 REFERRAL

Loaning your good name: You simply give someone the name and phone number of someone else whom you believe that person would benefit from meeting. All you're doing is allowing the other person to use your good name as a means of entry. You are leaving everything else up to them and actually chances are pretty slim they will even follow up.

Example: *You know John, as we were talking, I just thought of someone whom you need to meet. Paul Jones is a consultant who works . . . and there might be some ways you could help each other. Here's his phone number; give him a call and tell him I told you to call him.*

LEVEL 2 REFERRAL

Loaning your good name plus adding a note: In addition to loaning your good name and reputation, you also send an email or a personal letter to the other person saying nice things about the person with whom you're wanting to connect them (possibly including a bio which they e-mail you), and describing why you think the two would benefit from meeting.

Example: *You know John as we were talking, I just thought of someone who you need to meet. Paul Jones is a consultant who works . . . and there might be some ways you could help each other.*

I tell you what, send me your bio and some information on your company and let me send that on to Paul so he'll be expecting a call from you. Here's his phone number; give him a call after you receive my email and tell him I told you to call him.

LEVEL 3 REFERRAL

Loaning your good name, plus note, plus call: In addition to loaning your good name and writing a note or e-mail, you follow up that note with a personal phone call to further validate the person's character and abilities and the value you would see in arranging a meeting with the other person. The strength of a phone call from you might also eliminate the need for even sending a note or email. Sometimes this can be accomplished all in one step via a three-way phone call introduction.

Example: you would say the same as in example 2, but at the end you would add, *I'll tell you what John, I'll follow up the information I send on to Paul and then personally call and tell him a little bit more about you.* (If you have the ability to make a three-way phone call, just go ahead and do it right on the spot).

A Level 1 Referral might take you an extra five seconds on the phone; a Level 2 Referral may take 10 seconds to 30 seconds, and a Level 3 may take several minutes but if you will fit in several of these during the week, you won't believe what will start happening. The impact will be cumulative.

LEVEL 4 HOSTING

NetWeaving at its best: You arrange a meeting to introduce two or three persons to each other and you are there to moderate.

As good and effective as these referrals on the phone are, in practice, I have discovered that all of these first three pale in comparison to the fourth method of "NetWeaving referrals" which involves physically "Hosting" a meeting for two others.

WHY IS "HOSTING" A NETWEAVING MEETING SO SUPERIOR TO JUST MAKING A "REFERRAL?"

- With any of the other "referral" levels, you're leaving the work of setting up the meeting to the two others (although sometimes in Level 3, you can actually help set up the meeting at the time of the introduction). With "hosting," you are the one doing the work of setting up the meeting and it is work, with everyone's busy schedules and sometimes needing to address the questions of, "Why are you doing this?" and "How am I going to benefit from meeting this other person?"

- With "hosting", at the initial meeting, you give a little overview of why you felt the two persons would benefit from meeting each other, and explain a little about the whole NetWeaving concept.

- With "hosting", you are there to experience the magic and energy that flows forth, once the parties start talking. But what is most interesting is that in the majority of cases, the most significant thing or things the two people find in common, or the key benefits derived from being introduced, are not what you had assumed up front when you set up the meeting. They discover someone they know in common; or they find they go to the same church, or they belong to the same club, or uncover hobbies they have in common.

- After making introductions, giving a little overview of NetWeaving and why you brought the two persons together, you then get to sit back and just watch the magic. While moderating the meeting, you can use the same key questions (which we use when we set up NetWeaving cluster groups) to stimulate discussions of how each person may be able to help the other.

PIONTTO—THE BUSINESS VERSION OF "PAY IT FORWARD"

Towards the end of the meeting, after you have seen the magic of the two people looking for ways to help each other; you have introduced people to each other who have found things they have in common, you close the meeting by saying something along these lines:

I've probably had as much fun today and gotten as much out of this meeting as the two of you. But, now in exchange for what I've done putting this meeting together, there's one favor I'd like to ask for in return.

(You know the expectation is that you are going to ask for referrals for yourself. Instead you surprise them by saying):

I would only ask that in return each of you will agree to pay it forward and do what I have done and that is to host a meeting for two other people. We call this PIONTTO—Pass It On To Two Others. It's fashioned after the concept from the book, Pay It Forward, by Catherine Ryan Hyde, and the movie by the same name, in which Trevor, a seventh grade student, challenged by his school teacher to come up with something which will change the world, put it into action. The idea is that when someone does a favor for you instead of paying them back, you pay it forward by doing favors for three other people and so on and so on.

I hosted a meeting for the two of you, and now I'd like to ask each of you to host a meeting for two others and so on and so. It really could change the world . . . in a very positive way . . . and have a huge impact on business.

Now that you've seen the great things that happen when more people do NetWeaving, I hope you'll want to do the same thing I've done.

NETWEAVING "HOSTING" IS PERFECT FOR PERSONS IN TRANSITION

When someone is in between jobs, engaged in a job search, or is simply thinking of changing fields, the tendency is to look at it from a uni-dimensional viewpoint:

- Here's my track record—what I've done before;

- Here are my skill sets and strengths/weaknesses; and/or

- Here's what I'm looking for.

Will you hire me or do you know someone who might?

When we were differentiating networking from NetWeaving, we pointed out that there's nothing wrong with networking. It's just that when you are networking, you're typically doing so with your own needs in mind. When you're NetWeaving, you're also doing it with other's needs, problems, and opportunities laid next to your own. You're searching for both when you're NetWeaving.

We have shown a number of people who have been in transition (in between jobs) how and why it makes great sense for them to spend a good part of their time "hosting meetings" for persons whom they've known throughout their career. Think of what a difference it makes when you are not viewed as *someone looking for a job* but rather someone connecting others for those person's benefit.

Guess what else we are finding about hosting meetings and

what happens toward the end of most hosting meetings. One or both of the two persons who have been connected in the meeting turn to the NetWeaver who hosted the meeting and say, *"Now how can we help you?"*

MARK AND ANN SCHOOLER

In our other book, *"Power NetWeaving,"* I talked about Mark Schooler, one of the greatest NetWeavers I've ever known. Well, he may be challenged by his wife, Ann. Together they make quite a team. Either together or separately, they "host" eight to 10 meetings a week at their home.

Ann is an "in-demand" volunteer who helps non-profits. She doesn't charge for her services, which include such things as strategic direction and planning; board composition, structure, and conflict; event planning and fund-raising. Although she has a full load currently, she takes on new clients under two conditions: if she philosophically buys into the mission of the organization; and if she believes in the cause enough to put her own money into it.

How could a couple who spends virtually all their time connecting other people and hosting meetings; as well as finding resources for others, especially non-profits—be so financially successful? You just have to buy into the law of the universe that says, *the more you give, the more you get.*

This doesn't mean you don't have to also be on the lookout for ways to increase the chances that things will come back around to benefit you.

Both Mark's and Ann's work, along with their NetWeaving, generates many opportunities for creating abundant new healthy human relationships both in a personal as well as business context.

FOLLOW THROUGH AND FOLLOW UP

Where most people fail in their networking, as well as their NetWeaving efforts is in the follow through and follow up. I will touch upon the importance of follow up and follow through here and again in the chapter on forming NetWeaving cluster groups.

What good does it do to create meaningful dialogue with someone; began to build appreciation and acceptance for and from the other person; begin to bond, and then make the incorrect assumption that the details of the experience will stay with them for more than a day or so. Without follow up, follow through, and reinforcement, it will turn out to be just a pleasurable one-time experience.

The follow through begins right at the first meeting by doing such things as "repeating" the person's name several times—out loud—and again in your mind to try and solder it into our memories, or make an association to help us remember, or better yet, sneak over into a corner and make some notes on the other person's business card you have been given.

But following through by following up the next day becomes the most important step.

It used to be that all of us had some pretty good excuses for not writing thank you notes and note cards:

- *I'm out of note cards. I'll send one when I buy more.*

- *It will be several days in the mail before the person receives it and by then, they will probably have forgotten our conversation.*

- *It's just so hard to remember to do it.*

Now, with the internet and e-mail, these excuses go out the window. Personal handwritten note cards are still great, but if you can't do that, send an email.

By summarizing the key points you discussed during your meaningful dialogue (growth and learning exchange, plus NetWeaving), you are really enhancing your image and doing something almost no one else does.

You could also include:

- An article on an interesting topic you discussed or just some additional points to show you remembered some of the details of what you discussed.

- The names of people you discovered you knew in common or things or interests you found that you had in common.

- The names of people with whom you both agreed you might be able to connect each other.

- A list of resources you could provide each other.

By virtue of your follow up, you now become someone who means what they say and whose word can be trusted.

The appreciation and acceptance which began to build begins to develop into early-stage "trust," but you have to keep it going. The flame is lit, but it will die out over time without rekindling.

THE HEART OF THE PROBLEM

Most of us just don't create enough healthy "non-superficial" relationships as we go through the normal routine of our daily lives.

NetWeaving offers a way to do this within a business context that extends into our everyday lives. We won't get along with everyone we meet. By increasing the number of new contacts you make, the number of healthy new relationships you build will grow exponentially, as will the number of close and meaningful relationships over time. NetWeaving truly is contagious! Just watch. You will get better—both at the skills of being a connector of others, as well as becoming a resource for others. You will also become a better NetWeaving ambassador—spreading the word about this great concept, then watch how others begin emulating what you are doing—and respecting you for having encouraged them to do the same. Most people truly want to help others. They just need a little nudge.

9

CREATING NETWEAVING CLUSTER GROUPS

*Successful persons make a "habit" of doing those things
which failures refuse to do.*
— ALBERT E. GREY

W hy do people join groups? There are a variety of reasons but
the most common ones would include:

- To meet new people, socialize and make new friends.

- To gain acceptance from others—"I'm OK. . .you're OK."

- To expand their horizons and to learn from other people.

- To make personal, business, and social connections.

- To join together with others sharing common interests—garden, book, or bridge club.

- To join together to work on charitable, church, and

other "good works" projects.

- To assume some kind of a "leadership" role or to join in leading toward a goal or a cause.

From the first time I saw NetWeaving cluster groups in action, I knew they held great potential. And although we originally formed these cluster groups exclusively with the idea of NetWeaving in mind, we have now seen that NetWeaving can also be incorporated into any group formed for any of the above purposes and it will enhance the group's mission, whatever that might be.

The original idea behind a NetWeaving cluster group was to put six to eight people together with the sole purpose of exploring ways to get to know each other better, break through the typical superficiality and find ways to help each other. The idea was to create something that worked almost the opposite from what many "leads" groups are all about—"*I'll scratch your back; but you must also scratch mine.*"

Now there's nothing wrong with this and some people who will help form or be a part of a NetWeaving cluster group will also belong to some kind of "leads" or "referral" group in which you are participating in *expectation* of being given leads. They just need to make sure they come to the NetWeaving meetings with a different mindset.

In NetWeaving cluster groups, the idea is to enter primarily with the intent of helping other people by connecting them with people you know directly, or people who can lead them to others who can make favorable connections. It is to offer information and resources—our own plus those of others in our resource or contact network on a purely gratuitous basis—simply with the belief that some of your goodwill will pay off somewhere down the road. And it does, time and time again.

In some NetWeaving situations, you will benefit immediately. Nevertheless, it is often in the long-run where NetWeaving truly pays the biggest dividends. Whether the payback is short-term or long-term in coming, in almost every case the psychological and spiritual rewards, which come from helping others are immediate. In some cases, these rewards are as great as the financial rewards later on. So it is the **motives** as well as the **mindset** which differentiate NetWeaving cluster groups from leads and referral clubs and groups.

In NetWeaving cluster groups, the idea is to give, give, and give; share, share, and share, without expecting that any of your giving and sharing is going to come back. As someone said in an early group, *"I got out of a leads group I was in after attending several times because I felt too much pressure to make referrals to people who in some cases I didn't know very well, and to some whose quality of work I wasn't real sure of. What I really like about this NetWeaving group is that no one is keeping score."*

Now what will almost invariably happen in the real world, is that there will be some people who join the group who still don't get it! They will typically be quiet except when something comes up which would seem to be an opportunity for them to talk about providing their product or services. Over a period of time, these people will typically drop out because others will feel reluctant to share with them. When they don't see much or anything "coming back" to them, they leave.

But what uniquely sets true NetWeaving cluster groups apart from any other groups is that they are specifically designed to overcome the superficiality. Over time, they help to create and develop new healthy human relationships.

People within the group can sense a "genuineness" with others and therefore they want to get together outside of the group to get to know each other better and that's where the real relationships are formed.

HOW ARE NETWEAVING CLUSTER GROUPS FORMED AND WHY?

Whenever you put together a group of six to eight people who barely know each other and meet either one time only or several times over some extended period of time, chances are you will *bond* with a couple of them; create a good short-term or even longer-term relationship with one or two others, and then find that you have little in common with several others in the group—different personality and communication styles, belief systems, things in common, etc.

And yet most networking groups are formed **without** any fixed term agenda. That's especially true with some networking groups and organizations, who charge a fee for being a part of one. This gives people an economic incentive to stay in the group. Once again, there's nothing wrong with this and the money creates a form of commitment to the purpose which is to obtain as well as give out leads.

NetWeaving cluster groups are specifically designed to exist only over a limited period of time—to allow for those in the group simply to get to know others in the group well enough to identify the ones with whom they think they will eventually want to bond and create long-term relationships.

Back in high school and college, fraternities, sororities, service clubs, band, or any group served a similar purpose. They allowed us over time to see and experience persons in different social and communication situations, and we chose those persons from among the group with whom we really connected. Many lifetime connections were created during that period but it wasn't with the entire group, it was primarily with subsets within the group.

But, after families come along and with business pressures, especially in today's "time-stressed" world, we don't seem to find the time or the opportunities to make those kinds of deeper connections and many of the ones we make, stay at a relatively superficial level.

INCORPORATING NETWEAVING INTO ANY GROUP OR ORGANIZATION

I first experienced the magic and the energy of a group of people all focused on helping others rather than looking out only for how they might benefit, at a meeting of the Professional

Women's Roundtable in Pomona, California on 9/11. I knew then it was only a matter of experimenting with a number of different combinations to come up with some *best practices* for organizing and running them. We're still learning. Hopefully this book will inspire many others to experiment with entirely new NetWeaving cluster group models we never would have thought of.

The first set of cluster groups we formed was at an established business organization in Atlanta—the Buckhead Business Association (BBA). Based upon confidence shown by BBA leadership following a presentation I made to the Board, we initiated the first project in the fall of 2001, in the shadow of 9/11.

We learned many things from this first set of meetings and so what follows are suggested ways to form cluster groups based upon some things that worked well and things that didn't work so well. Some of these findings we've since incorporated in a project with the Metro Atlanta Chamber of Commerce as well as a project at the Buckhead Club, called "8 at 8"—in many ways fashioned with NetWeaving in mind.

The good news is that these cluster groups, even under the worst circumstances, will help initiate meetings and introductions which wouldn't have otherwise taken place. So long as you come out of one of these experimental cluster groups having met one or two people with whom you found you had things in common, and which you are now pursuing outside the context of the group, consider it a great success.

The real goal of NetWeaving is to expand the number of *new* healthy human relationships which you develop over a period of time, and these cluster groups are a great way to do that, so long as you and others are willing to give and give, and not keep score. Those who DO keep score will find very little comes out of the experience.

HOW TO FORM NETWEAVING CLUSTER GROUPS WITHIN AN EXISTING ORGANIZATION

As with any project of this kind installed within an existing organization, there must be total support and commitment from the leadership at the top. They must buy into the concept and philosophy and be willing to actively promote and support the project.

The project can be done at separate stand-alone events as we are doing at the Metro Atlanta Chamber of Commerce and at the Buckhead Club or they can be set up as a project of three or four meetings—typically one per month over a three to four month period with one person "hosting" a meeting for two others, and other work assignments in between.

The first step is usually to have someone within the organization make a 15-20 minute presentation on NetWeaving which can easily be done by using materials available in this book, as well as in the first book, "*Power NetWeaving*" (available at **www.nuco.com**).

Although we've tried a number of combinations in experimenting with the formation of NetWeaving cluster groups, we've found one design which seems to work the best—two or sometimes three persons who know each other well enough—determine they would like to get to know each other better and so they decide to form the "nucleus" of a NetWeaving cluster group.

FIRST STEP

The nucleus group (two or three persons) will have an organizational meeting where the principles and mission of the NetWeaving cluster group are discussed and established and they bring up the names of and some information about several other people who might be appropriate candidates to join the group. You should look for persons who are creative thinkers and who will challenge the group. Although you won't always know this ahead of time, try to pick people whom you believe are givers, not just *in it for themselves*. In short, they should be a person of character and someone who derives genuine satisfaction from helping others.

Although you certainly can create the groups totally from within the organization (members only), there is an advantage to inviting some or all of the additional persons to join from outside since it can become a great new member recruiting tool.

Any organization that sponsors NetWeaving cluster groups will find many people attracted to the concept and favorably impressed by a group who would foster this golden rule form of networking.

It is recommended that the group be no larger than eight since it often works out that two to three of the eight persons can't make it to any one meeting and that leaves five to six people in attendance at each meeting, which is just enough to let everyone really participate in the discussions and provide the time to get to know each other.

You can either approach persons whom you know well, or use this project as an excuse to approach someone whom you may only know slightly, or even not at all, but to whom you've been referred or just heard about from someone whom you know and would like to know better. Some groups may wish to "NetWeave" within their same industry, being careful to select persons not in direct competition with others in the group. Other groups may decide to go with a totally random selection from industries outside their own, with the only criteria to look for the most creative and free-wheeling thinkers.

HOW TO APPROACH SOMEONE TO JOIN YOUR NETWEAVING CLUSTER GROUP

If you were to approach someone whom you don't know well, here's an approach which you might use (or a condensed version of it):

(Let's say this is someone whom a friend of yours knows casually but just raves about what an outgoing creative thinker he or she is)

"Mary, you don't know me other than I believe you know Jack Jones who speaks very highly of you and calls you one of the most creative thinkers he's ever met. (important to get a reaction or response at

103

this point and maybe a little getting to know each other)

Through the (name of your organization) of which I'm a member, I'm involved in a very interesting program involving a new concept which is catching on around the country—called "NetWeaving." NetWeaving is a golden rule form of "networking" which is all about helping others . . . simply with the belief that, what goes around, comes around.

You, like many of us, have probably already have been doing some NetWeaving over your career, and just didn't have a good word to describe it, but this project is aimed at increasing everyone's awareness of and appreciation for the concept and is designed to get everyone doing a lot more of it which will be good for your business and just good for the world.

(Name of other person) and I are forming a six-person NetWeaving Cluster Group (at this point you could add a couple facts about your nuclear partner). We are each inviting two nonmembers to join our group to make a total of six persons. Your only commitment would be to attend a minimum of three two-hour meetings over the next four months. The idea is simply to get to know each other better over time; to brainstorm; to help each other: solve problems—business, family or personal; fill needs that each of us may have—once again in either a business, family or personal context, and to be a catalyst for any ideas or opportunities which each of us may have, but have never been able to get off the ground.

Assuming the meetings are scheduled when you are in town, would this be something which would be of interest and of value to you?

Obviously, a similar approach and explanation can be used to describe the project to someone you already know. The problem will not be in selecting your two non-member persons, but rather narrowing your choices down as to just whom you'd like to have involved in the project.

AGENDA FOR NETWEAVING CLUSTER GROUP MEETING NUMBER ONE

— MEETING ONE —
Developing or Enhancing Your Skills
as a Strategic Matchmaker

~ One of the persons will give a 15-20 minute overview of NetWeaving—this can be done by using a wide variety of materials available as well as a complimentary Power Point Slide Show available at www.netweaving.com.

~ Then, going around the table, each person will take 5-7 minutes to describe his or her business or position in a company and personal life, with the idea of explaining:

• What is their line of work—how do they make their money. . .or create revenue?

- If in sales or marketing, what does a best prospect for them look like and be very specific with a good bit of questioning here? Have him or her tell how they landed their best prospect? (We remember stories better than facts)

- What are their most burning issues—their "missing pieces"—in the form of needs, problems, and opportunities which they would like the other NWCG members to be out there looking for during their ordinary course of business?

- Do they have a "mission in life" or a "passion," and if so, what is it and how could the others be of help (people who have same passion, etc.)

- What is their "strategic advantage?"—important to be able to "sell" them and their services to others—What are their strengths? What differentiates them from their competition?

- What are the names of some people in town or in the organization whom they would most like to meet. Someone in the group may know that person or at least know someone who is close enough to make a valuable introduction.

- What is their family situation, any hobbies or any other interesting information they would like to share.

The real purpose of this session is help break through the superficiality and awkwardness we all go through as we're getting to know new people. It's only when people begin to feel safe and secure that they will begin to open up and share and it's then that the NetWeaving can truly begin.

- ~ Learning to be a better "connector" of other people involves learning to "listen with two pair of ears and two sets of antennae—one to be attentive for possible solutions to some of your own needs, problems, and opportunities, but a second pair/set to be attuned to those of others. Much of what you will be discussing and brainstorming within your cluster group is helping you see how you do this. You are simply carrying that same attitude and new listening ability out into your ever day conversations. When in doubt, throw out the question, "How can I help you?"

- ~ In preparation for the meeting, make sure to review the chapter on "referrals" and use the hosting and referrals notepad (in appendix) for a week and see how often on a telephone conversation you can remember to make a Level 1, 2, or 3 referral.

- ~ Assign or ask for a volunteer to be the "scribe". This is critically important. First, even good listeners don't retain much from information which is not written down shortly after hearing it. Secondly, good listeners will still get some of the information incomplete or wrong and so, writing the notes down, sending them out to each participant for corrections and additions, and then circulating the corrected notes will make a big difference in the group's total outcome. This not only helps people clarify things they may have misheard, but just as importantly, people will add points to the notes when they review them which are often more relevant and are stated in clearer terms than that which was mentioned during the meeting.

— ASSIGNMENT #1 —
HOSTING another NetWeaving Meeting for 2 others
(refer to Chapter on Hosting and Referrals)

For your first "hosting" meeting, it's best to "cut your teeth" by hosting a meeting for two people whom you already know well, and who trust you. You can be "strategic" in your matchmaking (meaning you're trying to match business opportunities for one or both of them) or "non-strategic." By that I mean that you can put two people together just because you like both of them— they are persons of good character, are interesting people, and are not self-absorbed, but would want to help others.

First you would call them and tell them a little about NetWeaving and you would like to play in the role of strategic matchmaker and introduce him or her to this other person over breakfast, lunch, or a drink after work.

They will almost surely agree to meet.

Also, as part of the next meeting on becoming a better

resource provider to others, have persons bring any articles or reference materials which they have found especially valuable in their personal and business life. This can be things like helping to become a better listener, motivational material, etc. Have each person make copies to be handed out.

AGENDA FOR NETWEAVING CLUSTER GROUP MEETING NUMBER TWO

— MEETING TWO —
Developing or Enhancing Your Skills
as a Resource Provider for Others

~ Review over any experiences which hopefully most or everyone has had in explaining and exposing other people to the NetWeaving concept. If you aren't using the word, and explaining NetWeaving to others, you're missing the boat. Get used to using the word on a daily basis and watch, as you explain it to others, how people light up to you.

~ Review any successful "matches" which anyone in the group made as a result of "hosting" a NetWeaving meeting for two other persons, or Level 1, 2, or 3 referrals people made over the telephone. It's not unusual to have a number of great stories just about the positive energy created during hosting meetings but there will also usually be a couple of examples where it really came to benefit one or both of the persons you hosted, and occasionally, there will even be some "immediate" payback to the NetWeaver to share.

~ Within the group, discuss and update any needs, problems, or opportunities anyone would like to bring up for others to be on the lookout for.

~ This meeting's agenda involves developing or expanding your skills as a strategic resource provider for others. If the Power NetWeaving book is being used, you can refer to the section in the book about how you develop and expand your skills as a resource provider, especially by sharing valuable internet websites you've learned about and how you are using them.

~ Share the resource materials each of the participants has brought and share how each has found this useful to them

— ASSIGNMENT #2 —
HOSTING another NetWeaving Meeting for 2 others

Last time we introduced you to the extremely powerful concept of "hosting" a meeting with two other persons:

Beginner Version—simply calling two friends, clients, or centers of influence whom you believe would benefit from meeting each other—in a business, family, or personal context and asking them to join you for a breakfast, lunch, or after-hours glass of wine. This was what you hopefully did for your first "hosting" meeting.

Intermediate Version—you know one of the individuals well, but only know the other person slightly or he/she may be someone whom you don't know at all, but who is referred to you by a good friend or close contact. In this situation, you will probably need to explain NetWeaving as to why you doing this, but have confidence because remember, you're doing it for their benefit, not your own, and people generally want to meet other people—especially if you do a good job of "selling" them as how and why they would benefit meeting the other person.

Advanced Version—you call one of your strongest and most talented clients and ask them if there's someone they haven't met but who they'd really like to know. Or, you may read an article in a paper or magazine about someone and decide for yourself that this person and your top client or friend would both really benefit from getting to know each other. In this case, you will need to do a good bit of fact-gathering about your client or friend because you will need to sell the other person, both on why you're doing this, and why they will benefit from meeting your friend or client. The good news is that powerful people want to meet other powerful and well-connected people.

Here's a rough script for the intermediate or advanced NetWeaving hosting meetings.

When you call the person whom you don't know well (or at

all), you would say something along these lines:

Joe, this is Bob Littell. We've never met, but I think you know (John Jones, whom I know through (where you know him from). Recently I told John about a good friend and client of mine, (Bill Jackson— name of your friend or client) who based upon what I know about you and from what John has told me, would be someone you would benefit from meeting and John agreed. (You will probably want to expand on this by bragging more about your friend or client).

I thought it would be great if I could get the two of you together. I'm sure that both of you would benefit and I'd simply like to act as the catalyst.

Also here you could explain a sentence or two about NetWeaving.

In case you're wondering why I'm doing this, I've become a strong advocate of a new concept which is really becoming popular called NetWeaving—which is all about "connecting" good people . . . simply with the belief that "what goes around, often comes back around." Besides that, I just enjoy connecting people and am always amazed at some of the things they discover between themselves— people they know in common, ways they can help each other, and also just because it's fun to do. Would you be able to have lunch with John and I sometime over the next couple of weeks, or would maybe an early breakfast work be better for you?

This will result in some great new contacts and eventually some great new clients and referrals, guaranteed.

You host the meeting, facilitate it, explain a little about the whole NetWeaving concept and after a successful meeting (virtually all will be) end it by saying something like this:

John and Mary (the two persons you hosted), I'm glad I was able to bring the two of you together today and from the sound of our conversation, it looks as if there are some things you have in common and several ways that you will potentially be able to help each other, or possibly collaborate. That's really what NetWeaving is all about—putting other people together in win-win relationships, with simply the belief on the part of the NetWeaver that, whatever goes around, comes around.

But in return for me putting together this meeting and hosting it, I would only ask for one thing in return—that sometime over the next several weeks or months, each of you will follow through on ways to help each other and that you will agree to do what I have done and host a meeting for two other people. This is what we call PIONTTO—Pass It On To Two Others—and now that you've seen the great things that happen when more people do NetWeaving, I hope you'll take me up on my request.

AGENDA FOR NETWEAVING CLUSTER GROUP MEETING NUMBER THREE

— MEETING THREE —
Developing and expanding Your Trusted Resource Network

1. Review over again any experiences which hopefully by now most or everyone has had in explaining and exposing other people to the NetWeaving concept as well as trying hosting and referrals. Have you now noticed how people "warm up" to you as you explain the concept?

2. Review any successful "matches" which anyone in the group made as a result of "hosting" a NetWeaving meeting for two other persons as well as "referrals" over the phone.

3. Within the group, discuss and update any needs, problems, or opportunities anyone would like to bring up for others to be on the lookout for. Creative brainstorming should now be fairly common and easy within the group.

4. This meeting's agenda involves developing or expanding your skills as a strategic resource for others by establishing and expanding your own "trusted resource network." Learning how to pick the right people; learning how to ask them to become part of your resource network; what should you expect in return?; How formal or informal should the relationship be? Refer to the chapter about creating a trusted resource network and moving potential candidates from the "Yellow Pages" level to the "Qualifying" level, to the "Trusted Resource" level. (See page 138)

— ASSIGNMENT #3 —
Followup on one of your Hosting Meetings

By now you should have hopefully held at least one "hosting" meeting and have seen the magic of serving in this hosting role. Although we can see how easy it is to actually put people together this way, we underestimate the value of it. We forget that putting together a meeting such as this takes work, and most people don't think of it from the standpoint of the value which they could gain and provide to others by doing this.

The assignment this time is to followup on the two persons whom you hosted and see if they have followed through with any of the needs, problems, opportunities, ideas, etc. which they discussed with the other person and with you present. Don't be surprised if the answer is "no" since everyone gets pulled back into their day to day crises but if you drop them both an email once again summarizing some of the things they discussed, and said they were going to do for each other, this will often help. Every time you help facilitate the relationship, your image is elevated in both party's eyes since you're doing it with their benefit in mind.

FOLLOW THROUGH AND FOLLOW UP

The most important benefits to come out of the cluster groups are not what happens at the meeting, but rather what happens in one-on-one meetings and "hosting" meetings which occur after or between the regular cluster group meetings.

That's why the role of the scribe who takes notes during the meeting and then circulates them for correction and circulation is so important to help people retain information and be able to remember connections they thought of at the time, but might have forgotten had it not been for the notes.

And as noted earlier, encouraging follow up "hosting meetings" is also a great way to grow "membership" within any organization. You meet someone within a cluster group with whom you find you have much in common. One or both of you discuss "hosting" a meeting for someone "outside" the organization and at that hosting meeting, you not only explain a little about NetWeaving and the hosting concept, but you can also point out that this is what your organization is promoting internally as a way to expand their member's networking in a truly effective way. The other person is usually truly impressed by this "win-win" approach to networking and will often decide to join.

Join a NetWeaving cluster group or help form one and you will be amazed at what eventually comes of it. Just remember that the purpose of the group is help "expose" you to more persons so that you can identify the few with whom you will eventually bond, or add to your trusted resource network.

**Sample Announcement from an Organization to persons
who signed up to be part of a NetWeaving Project**

TO: NetWeaving Participants
FROM: (Project Leader or President)
SUBJECT: NetWeaving Cluster Groups

Congratulations!

You have chosen to become part of a project which should have
beneficial effects not only on your business career and your personal life, but upon our organization as well.

NetWeaving is a golden rule form of networking which is
all about putting others' needs and interests on a more level
plane with our own. It reminds us how to be better "connectors" of other people for their benefit not our own, with the
belief that, "*what goes around. . .will come back around.*" It also
helps us learn ways that we can become a better "resource" to
others—either acting in that role ourselves—or assembling
what is referred to as a "*trusted resource network*".

We hope you will go into this project with the understanding and expectation of helping others and eventually
having good things come around to you. But also know that
the worst outcome . . . will be that you will get to know some
good people much better and that other people within our
organization will get to know you much better. And these
other persons, can help you find some of the "*missing pieces*"
to your own business, family, and personal jigsaw puzzles and

you, in turn, will hopefully be able to help them locate some of their own.

These missing pieces may be in the form of:

- needs which need fulfilling.
- problems which need solving or resolving.
- opportunities or ideas which need help or enhancement of some kind or they will always simply remain an unfulfilled idea or opportunity.

And any of these can be found in a:

- Business context (business, referrals, solution providers, etc.)
- Family context (help with a troubled child, daycare, etc.)
- Personal context (hobbies, travel, motivation and self-improvement, etc.)

You may have a secret "*passion*" which you can express to the group and they very well may have suggestions, connections, and information which can help you someday achieve your mission or allow you to pursue your passion.

You will become more conscious of and will be looking for opportunities to be a NetWeaver for others:

- Putting other people together in win-win relationships.
- Acting as a strategic resource for others—either acting in that capacity yourself, or beginning to create a wide and

deep resource network of others who excel at what they do, and share your gratuitous NetWeaving philosophy. In exchange for you agreeing to be part of their gratuitous resource network, they agree to be part of yours.

And eventually, many of you will become comfortable enough in the process where you will want to become a *"NetWeaving ambassador"* and take the concept out to other groups to which you belong. And that's really the ultimate goal of what NetWeaving is all about.

You have nothing to lose and everything to gain. Thanks for agreeing to be part of this important project.

10

Putting On A NetWeaving Event

The greatest discovery of my generation is that human beings can alter their lives by altering their attitudes of mind.
— WILLIAM JAMES

True Happiness. . .and Success. . .Lies More in the Giving Rather Than in the Taking

It's Saturday morning. You'd like to sleep in but you've committed to helping out working in a "soup kitchen" serving the less-fortunate. You drag yourself out of bed, get dressed and begrudgingly drive there. As you work the serving line and as you get to talk with some of the people and discover many of the unusual circumstances which drove them there, you change your perspective. These strangers become real people with faces and names who just need a helping hand and a lot of moral support. You leave that day, saddened by some of the stories you've heard and shuddering a little with a feeling of, *"there but for the grace of God go I."* But, unlike how you started the day, you are now totally energized by the small part you were able to play, a form of energy which can only be derived from the good feelings associated with helping others.

Getting people to participate in almost any charitable activity, which afterwards they talk about as one of their most enjoyable and rewarding experiences, is not always as easy as it would seem. In today's time-stressed world, most of us first set aside time for the things which we consider essential, and then fill in the remaining time slots with those activities which seem beneficial and/or enjoyable either from a business, family, or personal viewpoint.

Helping other people, in one way or another, is one of those activities which most people tend to look at as important, but not necessarily something which they are going to build into an every day habit. And yet anyone who has ever volunteered to help build a "Habitat for Humanity" house, or worked in a soup kitchen or spent a Thanksgiving helping out at a feed the hungry supper, will remember the good feelings that it evoked. And yet how many people do these kinds of activities more than once or twice a year, unless their company happens to be an active supporter and it's expected that they participate?

In a similar way, NetWeaving, with its focus first on helping others solve problems, identify and fulfill needs, and recognize and take advantage of opportunities, would seem to be one of those activities that would also fall into the category of doing it occasionally, but not necessarily on a daily basis. The rewards of NetWeaving, often provide "deferred" rather than "instant" gratification.

But as we've said before, because of the fact that some of your NetWeaving does result in immediate paybacks (enhanced image and a positive source of energy created), and because NetWeaving can be done in a "business" as well as a "personal" context, it can, with practice, easily be built into a daily habit and into your daily schedule, and can then become a springboard for other acts of gratuity and altruism.

The more NetWeaving you do, the more you want to do. It's truly contagious.

WHAT DOES A NETWEAVING EVENT LOOK LIKE?

In the article which appeared in the Atlanta Business Chronicle (October 11-17, 2002) and which is repeated pretty much intact as the foreword to this book, Jeffrey Gitomer, syndicated columnist, and nationally recognized speaker and author ("*The Sales Bible*" and "*Customer Satisfaction is Worthless, Customer Loyalty is Priceless*" see www.gitomer.com), said this about why the two NetWeaving events he attended were so powerful?

"*The results were fantastic. People spent hours trying to involve themselves in others' needs. To give of themselves first.*"... *Think about the power of it. In traditional networking, you show up to 'work the room' and try to make a few contacts. At a NetWeaving event, all the people in the room are trying to make connections for you.*"

NetWeaving events can come in all shapes and sizes, from a small gathering of 15 to 20 people, to several hundred or more. It won't surprise me that soon we will be holding

NetWeaving events at which thousands will attend. And I'd be the first to admit probably the most creative versions are still yet to be thought up.

In the larger of the two NetWeaving events which Jeffrey Gitomer attended we had seven "secret NetWeaving" judges sprinkled throughout the audience and at the end of the night, we awarded prizes to the persons whom the judges thought did the best job of NetWeaving for him or her during their conversations, either suggesting connections or resources which could help. Each judge selected one winner.

IT'S THE DIFFERENCE IN MINDSET THAT SETS NETWEAVING EVENTS APART

When people attend a typical networking event, they usually go with one idea in mind, to meet some potential prospects for what they have to offer. As we've said many times before, there's nothing wrong with this. We all need to look out for our own interests and networking events provide a way to cast our net very wide.

But those who come to a NetWeaving event are invited to come with a different mindset as well as a different set of goals. Sure we're still telling them to be tuned in for possible opportunity for themselves, but we stress NetWeaving is all about "helping others," with the belief and conviction that a payback will come somewhere down the road. This sets a different mood for the event. Therefore the questioning and the listening is focused externally on all the questions we've stressed in previous chapters: How they create revenue?; What does a best prospect for them look like? What is their most burning need, problem, or opportunity we might help them with? What is their strategic advantage that differentiates them from others who do the same thing or something similar?

As they are talking, rather than "qualifying" them as a potential prospect, as would be the case at a typical networking event, a skilled NetWeaver is sorting through his or her mental rolodex as the other person speaks to identify potential connections which could be made, or resources (their own as well as others) which could be suggested to fulfill needs; solve problems, and take advantage of opportunities.

AT A NETWEAVING OR A NETWORKING EVENT. . . THE KEY IS FOLLOWUP

The key to success in life usually lies in the small stuff. It always amazes me that we'll carve out large chunks of our time and our money to attend networking or NetWeaving events, and then will disregard the most important element to making it a success—the followup.

In Chapter 8, in which we covered "hosting" a meeting for others, as well as in Chapter 9, talking about forming NetWeaving "cluster" groups, we stressed the importance of having someone act as a scribe, both to get the key points down and circulate them for corrections and additions; and get them back to those in the group for reference and retention purposes.

Within a 24-hour period after meeting someone, especially if it's within a group setting where some of the conversations tend to "run together", you will lose 90 to 99% of what you heard, unless, within a fairly short period of time (one to 12 hours), you take good notes from your meeting or introduction.

A FOLLOWUP LETTER IS SOMETHING ALMOST NO ONE DOES

We mentioned it before, but it bears repeating. Some of the most creative and talented people almost always follow up a meeting with a "thank you" or enjoyed-meeting-you note.

How would you feel if you got such a note (especially since an e-mail makes this so easy to do) that read something like this.

Example:

John,

Really enjoyed meeting you last night at the XYZ Company NetWeaving event. I love this concept which really focuses on finding ways to help other people—both as a connector as well as a gratuitous resource provider . . . with the belief that "what goes around . . . often comes back around."

I have found that unless I take good notes within a fairly short time after speaking with someone and discussing how I might be of help, I tend to lose it for good.

From our conversation, here were some of the key points I heard you say which will hopefully help me in introducing or connecting you with people whom I know who might be able to help you.

You make your money by finding companies who are having problems with growth and are at that stage where they can't yet afford a full-time CFO type. A "BEST" prospect for you is one of these companies who typically have an outside accountant who does their books and their taxes, but who doesn't help much from a strategic and tax planning standpoint. You indicated what you consider to be your "strategic advantage" and what differentiates you from others is your broad experience track record which includes time with a large accounting firm, as well as having been CFO of a large as well as a medium-sized company. The other persons you have hired into your company also have a similar broad experience background.

Also, I remember that you said you really enjoy scuba diving and since my wife is a travel agent who specializes in "adventure travel", I've asked her to send you any information that comes across her desk on really interesting trips or vacations you may ever want to consider.

Please let me know if I heard you correctly and that this information is accurate. Also, if there are some other points which you didn't mention that night which would help me "sell" you better to someone I already know or someone whom I meet, please feel free to add to these notes and return them to me.

I already have a couple people in mind, but first I'd like to get together with you one-on-one and get to know you better. After I hear back from you, let's get together for breakfast or lunch over the next week or so.

Sincerely,

Sure, this is some additional work, but you will find that going this extra 1%, will make a 100% difference.

As Albert E. Grey once said, *"Successful people make a habit of doing those things that failures refuse to do."*

SOME EVENT EXAMPLES

Now let's look at a couple of events which people have done.

Jim Cichanski is someone whom I met when he attended a NetWeaving presentation I made at a church in Roswell, Georgia, to a group of "in-transition" managers and executives. Reverend Jack Pilger runs the program and it is really all about NetWeaving.

Jim, whose background has been in human resources, is CEO of a company called "Flex HR Inc." They provide part-time HR services for companies who have reached a size and growth stage where they need to ramp up their HR internal systems and procedures, but aren't ready to create an entire HR department.

Jim was attending this meeting at which I spoke on NetWeaving as a volunteer—looking for persons he could help connect for employment opportunities. Jim was "NetWeaving" before we ever met. Now that he has a word for what he's been doing, he will tell you, he is paying more attention to the skill sets, and consequently is doing 10 times as much as he was before.

Jim has held several NetWeaving events with neighbors, friends, and over 80 affiliate partners with whom he has made connections during the first year of his business. Over the course of the evening, while he serves, eats and drinks, he challenges the group to NetWeave among themselves. And about every 20 minutes or so, he gets everyone's attention and asks them to spend the next period of time getting to know someone else with whom they haven't yet talked. By the end of the night, most leave with a list of 15-20 "to-do's" which are all related to helping their new acquaintances.

Jim is now getting calls from some of those who have attended, as well as from others who hear about it, wanting to know when he is holding the next one.

ANOTHER EVENT EXAMPLE

Some of my close friends in Atlanta are the Harris'—Sydell, Arthur, Richard, and Karen Harris. They own and run what is now the largest day spa in the country, Spa Sydell. They are a wonderful family-owned business who not only challenge and inspire people to relax, reduce stress, and energize themselves by regular visits—massages, facials, as well as a series of relaxation treatments and procedures, but they volunteer a good deal of their own time to various charitable causes.

To help provide more visibility for their newest location in midtown Atlanta, I asked if they would want to "host" an "invitation-only" NetWeaving event. This was one of the two events which Jeffrey Gitomer attended and about which he wrote in his column. But what was unusual about this event was the power of the people who attended, all very successful persons from a variety of different industries and occupations.

Some persons have mistakenly believed that NetWeaving is most effective for younger persons just starting out who need to create and broaden their "contact networks". This event was living proof that high-level successful people gain just as much if not more from NetWeaving events, especially when they go in with the attitude of sharing their extensive network connections they have managed to accumulate over a very successful career, with other very successful people.

Probably most satisfying are the number of "post-event" connections on which people have followed up.

Mark Schooler in Dallas, Texas, perhaps the first NetWeaving ambassador, and first to pick up the concept and begin really spreading the word, took it to a friend, John Casey. By the time I was asked to come to make a presentation to their group, originally made up primarily of "in-transition" CEOs, they had taken the concept to heart to a point that they asked if they could actually call their group, "the Netweavers," which I readily gave them permission to do.

As they have expanded, they have added many more members

who are currently CEOs of active companies, but who are attracted by this what's-in-it-for-you, rather than what's in it for ME?

A FINAL EXAMPLE

One of the early adopters of Netweaving was the Atlanta office of UBS Paine Webber. After a warm reception to a couple of presentations I had made within the office, I was asked to help "kick off" a client appreciation reception several of the brokers hosted.

After giving the participants the opportunity to just engage in typical "small talk" for about the first half an hour, I was then introduced, and did about a 15-minute overview of NetWeaving, with the message everyone should now get back into their conversations with each other in a new mindset— "how can we help each other, either as matchmakers and connectors, or as potential resources for each other." There was great positive energy created as I drifted among the groups of people and listened to their discussions.

The feedback from the session was excellent and there is now a critical mass of NetWeaving ambassadors within the UBS Paine Webber firm who are now carrying forth the NetWeaving message in their everyday activities.

EVENTS IN SUMMARY

What has been most exciting about seeing the outcomes of

NetWeaving events is that people seem to be as "turned on" in this environment as they are in these other more altruistic (i.e. "charitable") situations. They also are more likely to attend and sponsor "business-oriented" NetWeaving events on a regular or semi-regular basis since they can see more visible benefits flowing back to them. This is especially true if they understand how to attend a NetWeaving event and that the key is the exposure to other like-minded people, and then following up with one-on-one meetings afterwards.

NETWEAVING FOR CHARITIES AND NON-PROFIT ORGANIZATIONS

Stop and think about the way most charitable fundraisers and donor appreciation banquets and receptions are organized. Typically the donors are invited to the event. They are informed about the great work the organization is continuing to do; probably told an inspirational story or two about someone who has been helped by their work, and then a plea is made for continued or increased donation support.

The networking part of the event is simply an informal gathering of donors who are left on their own to strike up any sort of dialogue they can think of with each other, which mostly ends up in small talk.

Why not precede the event with a letter thanking their donors and inviting them to the event? Invite them to come in a spirit of and with a mindset for NetWeaving, both to exchange ways they can help each other and/or find areas of commonality, as well as to brainstorm for creative ways to raise more funds for the charity or the organization. These key donors who are usually pillars of the community and successful in their own right, typically react to this NetWeaving challenge as if they've been given a work assignment. It allows them to skip the "small-talk stage" and move right into "meaningful dialogue."

It's also beneficial to break up the evening in different phases so that people have an excuse to get involved in several group discussions rather than just one. The idea is to help them make new connections, and to allow them to brainstorm with a fairly wide cross-section of the people in attendance.

So by introducing NetWeaving within the business community and then extending it into the charitable and non-Profit world, it not only helps create more business and more new interesting personal connections, it energizes people and makes them more likely to want to carry the NetWeaving message into their work for charitable organizations and non-profits with which they're already involved.

11

Building A
"Trusted Resource Network"

*Life is a series of experiences, each one of which makes us bigger, even
though it is hard to realize this. For the world was built to develop
character, and we must learn that the setbacks and grieves which
we endure help us in our marching onward.*
— Henry Ford

As you are mastering the NetWeaving skill set of becoming a
strategic connector of other people, you should also be working
on the second skill set which is learning how to be a better gratuitous resource provider to others. We spent a good deal of
time on becoming a better resource provider yourself and how
to better position yourself as one in the first book. Here we will
focus on the second important element of resource-providing—
learning how to build a network of other gratuitous NetWeaver
resource providers across a broad variety of industries, professions, and specialties.

Think of the names of several of the people whom you trust
the most. What are the characteristics which have inspired that
trust? Here are a few that come to mind:

- Over time, they have demonstrated a high degree of integrity and sense of urgency—they do things when they say they're going to do them and if there's a delay, they let you know so that it's not a surprise.

- They are very competent at what they do and with rare exception, the quality of the work they do or product they provide exceeds your expectations.

- There's an intangible bond that you feel with them that you can't completely explain, but whether it's chemistry or something else, you don't have it with that many other people.

- They have a positive mental attitude and a *can-do* spirit.

- You genuinely like working with them and enjoy their company.

How many people do you know who would possess all or almost all of these qualities? Not many?

One of my favorite business theories is espoused by Dr. Michael Mescon, former Dean of the College of Business at Georgia State and well-known author, speaker and consultant. In his book, *Showing Up For Work and Other Keys to Business Success* he describes his "minimum shaft expectation theory." Dr. Mescon observes that in the somewhat jaundiced world we live in today and experience as consumers, we enter into almost any transaction, whether it's buying a car, getting the air conditioning in our house fixed, or utilizing a service, with the expectation that somehow we're going to get shafted.

- The product won't work as we anticipate; there will be hidden costs or charges we didn't understand up front; or the service will probably be below our standards.

And so we relegate ourselves to the fact if we come out of the deal not feeling too worse for wear from our experience, feeling **we haven't gotten shafted too badly**, we come out feeling OK.

It's sad, but generally true. But as Dr. Mescon points out, that's also the great news for those whose product or service consistently exceeds expectations. *"You can carve out market share in no time when you under-promise and over-deliver."*

CREATING A TRUSTED RESOURCE NETWORK

Now imagine for a second that your only goal in life is to recruit a network of persons—across all industries, products and services—that fall within the criteria listed at the beginning—and they would become your "trusted resource network."

Think of a "trusted resource" as being someone who when you refer that person to someone else, and after the product is used or the work is done, the person to whom you referred your trusted resource is so grateful he or she not only thanks you, but gets down on their knees and thanks you, either because the product worked so well, or the service performed was well above expectations, or both.

Why then aren't all of us constantly in a recruiting mode for persons who can fill in the gaps in our trusted resource network? Partly it's because we never thought about the idea of recruiting a *Trusted Resource Network*. Secondly, even if we have created an informal network which we've formed over time, we tend to think too narrowly. Thirdly, outside of our own field of knowledge and expertise, finding "*best of breed*" persons takes some work. You want to separate those who **talk** a good game about their expertise and the quality of their work, and those who are truly exceptional.

Third-party referrals and outside recognition by acknowledged experts in that field are the best way to determine this.

Top real estate agents are often easily identifiable. And not surprisingly, most have become tops in their field by NetWeaving—just without a good word for it. They are natural connectors of other people: buyers with sellers, tenants with landlords, leasees with leasors. They are typically great information resources themselves. But on top of this, the best ones have truly assembled a wide and broad network of "trusted resources" in a wide variety of industries and specialties.

Say you're in the market to buy a home and you have a thousand questions:

- Are there good medical facilities close by and do you have the name of an outstanding pediatrician?

- How about the name of a great vet?

- We see several things we want to change about the house. Do you know a great remodeler?

- Who gives the best ballet lessons in town and where is the facility?

Now, an average or below-average real estate salesperson would probably still have names of contacts or could readily find answers to any of these questions and many others. But if some of the referrals didn't turn out to be that great, no big deal, the house has been sold and who knows, they may never see that person again.

But a great real estate agent or broker has a *Trusted Resource Network* made up of persons who, over time, have proven their salt. The homebuyer not only becomes a vocal advertisement for the way the sale of the house was handled but the real estate NetWeaver has earned a reputation as being a walking, talking yellow pages directory when it comes to resources and not just "average" references, but each one— tops at what they do.

And guess whose reputation also gets elevated as a result of making the referral of a "trusted resource"? You guessed it—the real estate person who now earns the reputation of being a "USA CARP" (a Universally Sought-After Connector And Resource Provider).

ANOTHER FALLACY OF TRADITIONAL NETWORKING—REFERRALS

People who go to networking events expecting to get leads and referrals for business are often disappointed. And even when they are given leads, they are normally not very effective leads. After all, without knowing very much about the individual to whom you might be referring someone:

- Their skills, talents, and knowledge;

- The quality of their work;

- Their reliability and sense of urgency;

- Their follow through; and

- Their integrity.

Who would be willing to risk some of their most valuable relationships with friends, clients, and centers of influence without knowing about some or all of their attributes?

THE PROCESS OF CREATING A TRUSTED RESOURCE NETWORK—FROM YELLOW PAGES. . . TO QUALIFIED. . .TO TRUSTED RESOURCE

We refer to someone whom you meet for the first time at an

event, meeting, or just any first time introduction, as a "yellow pages" level referral, meaning all they are is a name, company, phone number, and some information about what they do. There's no trust and no relationship established yet.

One of the main goals you should set for any networking event you attend is to identify several "yellow pages" level, *potential* future additions to your trusted resource network. These are persons who impress you enough that you want to learn more about them and continue to "qualify" them.

In some cases, the person who introduces you to this person is someone whose opinion you already trust and value. When they begin raving about how good and reliable this person is at what they do, and if you feel the same way after you visit for awhile, you may want to actually start them at the next level, the *qualified resource* level.

At this level, either you have now done *some* business with them—referred them to someone and you liked the feedback you got, or they were referred to you by someone whose opinion you genuinely trust and they are sincere in their praise of the person referred to you.

You then continue to "test the waters" with him or her and eventually you either decide to keep them where they are (or lower them back to the yellow pages if they disappoint you), or you've seen enough that you decide to add him or her to your trusted resource network.

WHEN YOU'RE RECRUITING YOUR TRUSTED RESOURCE NETWORK. . . YOU ACT LIKE A SEARCH FIRM

When you are searching for persons to be added to your best-of-breed" trusted resource network, you change roles. Your reputation is on the line when you make a referral and so you become a "headhunter" searching for the most qualified person to fill each vacant slot. You have to be very careful in your selection process if you really want to make your network as powerful as it can be. If you put it together in the right way and get the right people involved, it can become a tremendous reflection back on you.

And when you ask someone to join your trusted resource network, it can be a real honor to that person when you explain the concept and give them the criteria you used to select them, as well as some of the names of the select people included (some whom they probably know). And guess what? That person will perform better for you knowing that he or she is part of a select group chosen for their excellence at what they do.

You should also encourage them to form their own network and you should volunteer to be one of their gratuitous resources if they feel you can qualify.

INTRODUCE YOUR TRUSTED RESOURCE NETWORK TO EACH OTHER AND ACROSS OTHER PERSON'S TRUSTED RESOURCE NETWORK

As you build your trusted resource network and as you teach others how to do the same, you create new opportunities. First, when you introduce members of your trusted resource network (best-of-breed individuals) to other's trusted resource network, they will make connections that will come back to benefit you.

Secondly, by helping others create and expand their own trusted resource network, you occasionally can "borrow" one from their network and vice versa.

One of the best ways to create and/or expand your trusted resource network is by being involved in small study groups or NetWeaving "cluster groups" as we covered in Chapter 9.

EXAMPLE OF INVITING SOMEONE TO JOIN YOUR TRUSTED RESOURCE NETWORK

Here is a hypothetical approach you might use in asking someone to become part of your trusted resource network.

Mary, we've known each other for some time now and I've been very impressed by (say those things which have impressed you—quality of work, attention to detail, sense of urgency, reliability, organization or management skills, etc.) as a (their occupation and specialty). *You may or may not have ever heard of a term called NetWeaving, but it's a 'golden rule' form of networking which is all about helping other people simply with the belief that, 'what goes around comes around.' In addition to becoming a better "connector" of other people for their benefit not our own, NetWeaving talks*

143

about being a 'gratuitous resource' for others—either acting in that capacity ourselves or assembling what is called a "trusted resource network" made up of persons who are "best of breed" at what they do and share your same NetWeaving philosophy.

As you assemble a wide and deep trusted resource network, your value to your clients, friends, and centers of influence is enhanced by the value of this broad and deep network you have put together.

Based on what I've seen and the work that you've done for some of my (friends, clients, centers of influence), *I would like to ask if you would consider becoming part of my Trusted Resource Network?*

All that is involved is agreeing that for some basic questions and issues which involve your area of specialty, I will occasionally refer clients or prospects to you, knowing that you will give them the best possible advice and direction—and not charge for the first couple of things that you do for them even if they offer to pay you. (They probably have already been doing this for you).

In exchange, I will agree to do the same for you and some of your clients so that we end up becoming part of each other's trusted resource network, assuming that is a role you'd like me to play.

Put together carefully and being very picky about who you invite to join, your trusted resource network—formal or informal—can end up being your greatest sales tool or simply a mechanism for better serving others.

TRUSTED RESOURCE NETWEAVING EXERCISE

- List the names and occupations/professions of all the

person whom you would consider to currently be part of your "trusted resource network."

- Think of all the occupations/professions missing and stop and think of the names of some persons whom you like but don't know well enough yet to add to your trusted resource network.

- Add these to your "mental rolodex" of persons for whom to be on the lookout.

- Let others know that you're looking for the best person in a particular field and ask if they know the names of one or two.

- Have a reception once a year where you invite all the members of your trusted resource network to NetWeave with each other.

12

NETWEAVING INSIDE COMPANIES
AND ORGANIZATIONS

Neither fire nor wind, birth nor death can erase our good deeds.
— BUDDHA

Quite some time ago, while attending a Metro Atlanta
Chamber of Commerce meeting which featured a panel discussion and workshop on providing superior customer service, an
entirely new avenue and application for NetWeaving materialized. From what I saw and heard, I believe this "internal" form of
NetWeaving can apply in any corporate setting, as well as within
any organization where two or more people are employed.

After the three panelists made their opening remarks, each
who either ran or was with a company specializing in CRM
(customer relationship management), the room of a little more
than 50 people was divided into three separate groups and sent
to separate rooms with the same assignment: come up with the
number one **barrier** within companies that thwarts good customer service from taking place, as well as the number one **contributor** to providing good customer service.

In the breakout room of about 15 people to which I was assigned, it turned out I was the last person polled on his opinion and answers for each of the two questions posed. After about the first seven or eight persons around the room had provided their answers, most of the others were agreeing or modifying an answer previously stated.

When it came my turn, I threw out somewhat of a curve. Taking part of a page from Abraham Maslowe's hierarchy of needs theory, I observed when I had been on the corporate side, and in most other organizations with whom I'd worked or consulted (including the U.S. Government where I interned for several summers during college), the number one "barrier" to providing good customer service I saw was defensive or uncooperative behaviors between and among various areas of the company or organization caused by "territoriality" concerns and issues.

Maslowe would probably interject something to the tune of, once food is on the table, and safety and survival issues are mostly handled, the next most basic human drive is "territoriality" and that doesn't just mean "turf" in a real estate sense. Territoriality can mean anything that I consider to be "mine" which could include:

- My responsibilities or duties.

- My span of control or chain of command.

- My authority over an area or a position on the organization chart.

In other words, it boils down to "control" and "power". And these "territoriality" concerns extend from the chairman, president and CEO level all the way down to the mailroom clerk, the janitor, and any new employee who has been with the company long enough to recognize where he or she stands in the "pecking order".

Therefore, assuming good operations and efficient systems are in place, these "territorial" walls or "silos" are the next greatest barriers which thwart cooperation and coordination between departments or divisions in the company, and this almost inevitably translates into poor customer service— *"That's not my job—try calling this person."*—pass the problem on to the next person, or, *"If I help you solve the problem, you (or your area) will get credit for it. . .not me (or my area)."*

How much more productive do you think any company would be if their employees, from top to bottom, were constantly looking for ways to help each other, rather than consciously or subconsciously sabotaging cooperation?

This could include sharing leads from one division to another as well as understanding more about other departments and divisions and being on the lookout for ways to help bring them more business or make suggestions for streamlining their operations.

All of these extend to providing better customer service. Where there is harmony and cooperation between and among departments and the silos and territorial walls are either torn down or at least minimized, the customer is provided superior service.

But too many times, the attitude which permeates the

organization is, "we win only if they lose;" or if we help them look too good, will that somehow come back to make us look less good?

In our group, I proposed this "territoriality" problem as what I thought was the Number 1 barrier to good customer service, and then after giving a brief overview of NetWeaving, suggested that creating an internal culture of NetWeaving within the company, would be the Number 1 way to promote good customer service.

Not only were my two suggestions adopted and voted upon by our smaller breakout group, but when assembled back in the main meeting room, and after each of the groups presented their recommendations, my two suggestions—both for the Number 1 barrier (i.e. the primary cause of poor customer service), as well as the top "solution" (creating more an atmosphere and culture of NetWeaving) were both selected.

SO HOW DO YOU DO THIS?

I am not a CRM expert and would prefer to stick to my chosen path in helping promote NetWeaving in the *external* world rather than *internally* within corporations and organizations. Nevertheless, some CRM specialists with whom I've spoken, totally agree with this assessment—how creating more an internal NetWeaving culture can help tear down territorial walls and silos. Several are already beginning to tackle this side of the equation. I believe that once a number of CRM experts recognize that by simply giving this potential solution a "name"—NetWeaving—and identifying successful "skill sets" on the inside, as I have hopefully done on the outside, it can create an awareness that will translate into concrete strategies to facilitate this within any company or organization.

I like to equate this "internal NetWeaving process" to a "365-day softball team," since in many ways, it's really just all about getting to know each other on a more personal level, rather than that guy "Ralph" in accounting, or that woman "Suzie" in Purchasing. The larger the organization, the more difficult this is, but the good news is that when it starts taking hold, it tends to be contagious.

So if you are on the CRM side, I hope you will take up the "internal NetWeaving" challenge and seek to find the answer to the question:

"How can we create an atmosphere and environment of NetWeaving which will help tear down. . .or at reduce. . .some of the NATURAL territorial walls, with its accompanying "defensive" behavior which we should anticipate, rather than be surprised by?"

There's no question that this is a long-term process, but if we can begin to create new ways to promote NetWeaving on the "inside" of companies, organizations and institutions, I'm convinced we will have some of the same positive results we are seeing on the "outside" with NetWeaving and the impact on overall productivity and profitability could be significant.

13

It's The Relationships, Stupid! Or How NetWeaving Can Increase Your Chances Of Being Lucky— How To Attract Good Luck

Between ourselves and those who cross our path. . .
chance spins an invisible thread of awareness—a luck line.
— A. H. Z. Carr

WHO MAKE THE BEST NETWEAVERS?

In Chapter 6, we discussed how relationships are nurtured, culminating in trust, and then maintained and strengthened over time by good follow up and follow through.

We also observed that some people seem to have a natural advantage in initially gaining acceptance due to qualities or attributes we don't fully understand and whose underlying nature may be partly biological, genetic, and neurological in nature. Psychological and sociological factors developed during our upbringing, especially in early childhood, also play a part.

You don't need to explain to someone who has raised a large family and who in spite of attempting to raise them the same, has seen an amazing range in personalities, that there are underlying factors at work which are largely out of our control and which account for many of the differences.

Although there are many different personality dimension grids and models, I find they all pretty much fall into the same five, six, or seven personality types:

Amiable—friendship being most important—*"Why can't we all be friends?"*

Analytical—problem-solving—*"Why am I thinking what I'm thinking?"*

Artistic—expressive—sensory—*"The whole world's a stage . . . beauty is in the eye of the beholder."*

Assertive—take charge—"The stuff that Type A's are made of—*"If you're not ready to lead. . .then get out of the way."*

Extrovert—adventuresome, gregarious—*"Have you heard the one about?"*

Introvert—shy—passive—*"I'm perfectly content with being by myself and curling up with a good book."*

Responsible—conscientious—*"I must finish everything on my* *plate because that's my responsibility."*

One thing that all of these personality types have in common is that to a greater or lesser degree, they all need to establish relationships with others. The amiable, assertive and extrovert types have a much easier time than the analytical and introvert types in doing so. I've observed that the artistic and the responsible types are more neutral when it comes to ease of "relationship building" although there are wide variations and some of these types are also some of the best relationship builders.

Not only are there many different versions of these personality types, in reality, most of us are mixtures of some or even all of these. Although some models suggest we all have one dominant overriding personality characteristic, I believe this can also be *situational* and depending upon the circumstances, we can change our dominant characteristic and even have more than one dominant characteristic operating at the same time.

The analytical personality tends to like to problem solve and also likes to be seen as dependable and responsible. He or she doesn't feel comfortable in the extrovert role. The extrovert in many cases likes to be the center of attention and sometimes the facts and solutions tend to be less important than the delivery or in the attention which their actions engender.

The personality elements of extroversion and introversion represent an interesting contrast in trying to decide who might be more "natural" NetWeavers.

On the surface, your "knee-jerk" answer to the question of which group—extroverts or introverts—would be better at

NetWeaving would probably be "extroverts" since we think of those who are "glib and gregarious" as the ones most likely to excel at this relationship-building skill.

I would like to suggest that Netweaving is the ultimate "equalizer"—enabling those persons, who see themselves as semi-introverts and highly analytical, to equal or even surpass their more outgoing counterparts.

Analyticals tend to dislike being seen as too pushy and sales-y. They get their satisfaction out of problem-solving and acting as a resource for others. Guess what? These just happen to be the two key skill sets of NetWeaving and once these more analytical and introverted persons see that what others may perceive as a weakness to actually be a strength, their self-confidence soars.

Many movies in the 90's, before the technology bubble burst, carried this message about a world which would be totally ruled by "techies"—remember "Revenge of the Nerds?" And remember the joke, "*What do you call the guy in high school, who 10 years ago carried the slide rule and had 10 pens and mechanical pencils holstered in his pocket protector*? "*BOSS.*"

During that over-exuberant dot.com period, some interesting things happened. Anyone who could "talk technology" could run circles around their non-techy "bosses" who grew up in the old school where only relationships counted. These young turks were seen as the new geniuses who would soon control the world. When the tech bubble burst, those same "old school" bosses were now firing and laying off some of these "*boy and girl geniuses*" who understood technology, but didn't really understand the importance of or how to build and maintain relationships.

But then when the economy even turned worse, some of those bosses who had let the young turks go, joined them in the ranks of the unemployed because no one really had made the point clearly enough to leaders of industries and the investors pouring money into technology that the real challenge and the ultimate solution was to strike a balance.

Technological savvy is needed more than ever to achieve cost-savings, productivity efficiencies, and expanded sales and marketing results, but building and maintaining relationships is just as important as it has ever been and must be "woven" into both sides of the equation.

Not that long ago, some "technocrats" in the insurance and banking industry world sincerely believed that in that new world of technology, people would gladly sidestep insurance agents. Armed with ways to get on the web they would calculate how much insurance they should own, and then eagerly shop for the very lowest premiums, and buy what they needed—maybe even more—now that they wouldn't have to fool with those annoying (what many saw as pesky) insurance agents.

Some in the automotive industry saw a world where persons would go on the internet do all their shopping, and then simply order their cars.

Many in the real estate industry shared a similar vision where persons would simply do a visually "web-enabled" "walk-through" of houses that fell within their specified criteria and someone would simply be needed to do the closing once they had chosen the house.

Now, I'm not suggesting that things are going back to where they were 10 or 15 years ago. In fact, I actually believe that when all the dust settles in another five to 10 years, when the "*world goes visual,*" when the picture phone is a reality, there will be a middle ground between a personal meeting and a voice-only telephone conversation. But relationships will still be king and technology will just allow us to build and maintain them in new and more creative ways.

Regardless of your personality type or combination thereof, I believe if you will incorporate NetWeaving into your daily habits—begin listening and being tuned in with a second pair of ears and antennae, and to always be on the lookout for other person's missing pieces to their business or personal jigsaw puzzles—you will learn how to build more new healthy human relationships than you ever thought possible. And in addition to becoming successful beyond your wildest dreams, you will achieve a satisfaction with life unlike anything you've ever experienced. And that will make you want to become a "NetWeaving ambassador" and to spread the word to others.

Who knows, as the whole world discovers the wonders of NetWeaving and as more people begin hosting a couple of meetings a week for others on a regular basis; begin making referral connections on the phone, by e-mail, and in person; begin forming NetWeaving cluster groups and holding NetWeaving events to help break through the superficiality, and spreading the word so that others will do the same—*we may just change the world.* And wouldn't that be something.

INCREASING YOUR CHANCES OF BEING LUCKY

At a NetWeaving meeting hosted by a friend, Ken Hilber, whom I met through another friend, Lew Schiffman, I met Joe Wolfe. Lew had met Ken at a party and just thought Ken was someone I should meet. He was right and today we continue to NetWeave for each other. Joe and I have gotten together a couple of times since and there's no doubt in either of our minds that we will stay connected for a long time and find ways to help each other. But Joe has already been a great NetWeaver for me, as a resource provider, without even knowing it.

Joe gave me a copy of a book, written all the way back in 1952, by AHZ Carr (Wilshire Books)—*"How To Attract Good Luck."* It's a short, easy read, which is loaded with common sense principles and ideas.

Nevertheless, there was one part of the book which when I read it, it struck me like a bolt of lightning and how it ties in perfectly with NetWeaving.

Mr. Carr states, and I'm paraphrasing a slight bit, *"The first step in attracting good luck is to understand that most of our good luck* (he defines as *"the beneficial effect of chance upon our lives"*) *comes to us through other people".*

"To expose ourselves to luck, then means in essence to come into healthy human relationships with more people."

"Between ourselves and those who cross our path, chance spins an invisible thread of awareness—a luck line"

"The more luck lines you throw out. . .the more luck you'll find."

So if you want to increase your luck, you simply need to

increase the number of healthy human relationships you create because as you do, in each and every case, you activate a "luck line".

I can honestly promise (and I'm not alone here) that since I've truly become more aware of NetWeaving, started making referrals on a daily basis; begun hosting at least a couple meetings a week; continued helping set up NetWeaving cluster groups of all kinds, sizes, and shapes, and especially since I've been out spreading the word about NetWeaving's "win-win-win-win" benefits, I have developed more new healthy human relationships over the last year than ever before, **easily by a factor of 10.**

You can, too. And you will find it just as rewarding and energizing as I have. This is because it is so true that, "good things happen when good people make things happen". . . that's because "what goes around, really does come back around."

NetWeaving Notepad

Date_____

Conversation with:_____

☐ In Person   ☐ On the Phone   ☐ By Email   ☐ Other _____

TYPE OF NETWEAVING ACTIVITY

Level 1 Referral – While on Phone or in Direct Contact:
Offer name of ANOTHER person: _____
who would benefit from knowing this person
Their phone number: _____

Level 2 Referral – While on Phone or in Direct Contact:
Offer name of ANOTHER person: _____
who would benefit from knowing this person and promise to Email or write note
to them plus send other info (e.g. bio of the person) as way of introduction.
Their phone number: _____

Level 3 Referral – While on Phone or AFTER Direct Contact:
Offer name of ANOTHER person: _____
who would benefit from knowing this person AND make phone call to the OTHER
person (3-way phone call if possible) as way of introduction.
Their phone number: _____

Level 4 Hosting a Meeting – Set up & host meeting to introduce 2 or 3 other persons:

Name: _____   Phone: _____

Name: _____   Phone: _____

Name: _____   Phone: _____

☐ **Refer Someone as a Resource** Name

Impressed enough by this person, consider as possible future "Trusted Resource"

Name: _____   Phone: _____

Resource Category or description: _____

Followup Dates: _____   _____   _____   _____

Good things happen. . .when good people MAKE things happen.